Solving the Puzzle

Solving *the* Puzzle

A Student's Guide to Historical Research and Writing

VALERIE S. THALER

broadview press

BROADVIEW PRESS
Peterborough, Ontario, Canada

Founded in 1985, Broadview Press is a fully independent academic publishing house owned by approximately twenty-five shareholders—almost all of whom are either Broadview employees or Broadview authors. Broadview is supported by a collaboration with Trent University, a liberal arts university located in Peterborough, Ontario—the city where Broadview was founded and continues to operate. Broadview is committed to environmentally responsible publishing and fair business practices.

Library and Archives Canada Cataloguing in Publication

Title: Solving the puzzle : a student's guide to historical research and writing / Valerie S. Thaler.
Names: Thaler, Valerie S., author.
Description: Includes bibliographical references and index.
Identifiers: Canadiana (print) 2025016969X | Canadiana (ebook) 20250169703 | ISBN 9781554812820 (softcover) | ISBN 9781460405727 (EPUB) | ISBN 9781770486133 (PDF)
Subjects: LCSH: History—Research. | LCSH: History—Methodology. | LCSH: Academic writing.
Classification: LCC D16 .T43 2025 | DDC 907.2—dc23

Broadview Press handles its own distribution in Canada and the United States:
PO Box 1243, Peterborough, Ontario K9J 7H5, Canada
555 Riverwalk Parkway, Tonawanda, NY 14150, USA
Tel: (705) 482-5915
email: customerservice@broadviewpress.com

Broadview Press books are imported and distributed in the United Kingdom and European Union by:
Gazelle Book Services Ltd.
White Cross Mills, Hightown, Lancaster, Lancashire, LA1 4XS
sales@gazellebookservices.co.uk

European Union – Responsible Person (for official use only):
eucomply OÜ
Pärnu mnt 139b14
11317 Tallinn, Estonia
hello@eucompliancepartner.com
+33757690241

Canada Broadview Press acknowledges the financial support of the Government of Canada for our publishing activities.

Developmental Editor: Maxwell Uphaus
Edited by Michel Pharand
Book design by Em Dash Design

PRINTED IN CANADA

1 2 3 4 5 6 7 8 9 10   25 26 27 28 29 30

CONTENTS

Additional practice exercises are linked throughout the book and can be found at sites.broadviewpress.com/puzzle/
Passcode: 49lfsw8

Preface

I originally wrote *Solving the Puzzle* after many semesters of teaching first-year college students at Towson University in Maryland, where our focus was to research and write short history papers. My ultimate goal was to help students learn to think critically. Even if they never planned to take another history course in college, the skills they learned in this course would still apply elsewhere. Having created the course and improved upon it each term to meet students' learning needs, I felt it would be worthwhile to share the insights I'd derived from it with other students and faculty. At the heart of *Solving the Puzzle* is a step-by-step methodology for teaching students how to investigate the past using clear-eyed, logical reasoning.

Students who successfully completed the research process—navigating all of its twists and turns—were usually very glad they stuck with it. At the end of the semester, they knew they had tackled intellectual challenges that surfaced along the way and felt a sense of accomplishment. They had avoided the easy shortcuts that in the past allowed them to get a passing grade but didn't help them mature as critical thinkers.

Today, it is even more tempting for students to cut corners when assigned a research paper. The most significant technological advancement in the last decade has been the rapid growth of generative AI (Artificial Intelligence). In November 2022, Open AI released ChatGPT, a conversational bot that, in seconds, can search online databases and generate papers according to students' preferences. Not surprisingly, professionals in the field of higher education differ on how to respond to the rapid growth of AI, and responses vary a great deal depending on the academic discipline, the particular course, and the nature of the assignment. Faculty now incorporate policies on AI into their syllabi, and some rely on AI detection tools (which have varying degrees of reliability) when evaluating student work.

Faculty need to develop AI policies that help students understand the proper role for AI in the history classroom. Used responsibly, AI can be an indispensable tool for students as they seek to gather data from a wide range of sources across the internet.

Instructors also should provide clear guidelines for what constitutes inappropriate use of AI, such as in the construction of thesis statements, the analysis of sources, or the writing of historical essays. As history educator Julianna DeSilvia writes, "The new focus [of history classrooms] need not be on the collection of knowledge, but on the appraisal of resources and data." Students need to know how to question sources, examine questions of bias, and evaluate the reliability of the information they read. Since AI can *itself* be weaponized to produce "deepfakes" and other forms of disinformation, developing critical thinking skills is even more important today than it was when I was teaching the courses that gave rise to this book.

In an age of hardening political and social divisions, extreme voices often speak the loudest. The year 2025 requires our young adults to be wise, discerning consumers of information who approach every source with some level of skepticism. We all need refresher courses in media literacy—guidelines on figuring out how to distinguish "real" news articles from the "swamp of misinformation" that lives on the internet.[1]

At their best, history classrooms—and historical writing—model reasoned, thoughtful, and nuanced discussion based on sound interpretation of sources. History instructors teach communication and thinking skills that are desperately needed in our polarized culture. The digital companion to *Solving the Puzzle* will emphasize these real-world applications of the skills taught in each chapter.

Valerie Thaler
April 2025

---

1 See Julianna DeSilvia, "AI in History Classrooms: How Artificial Intelligence can Foster Genuine Learning," *Historica Blog*, March 14, 2024, https://www.historica.org/blog/ai-in-history-classrooms. On "swamp of misinformation," see Frank Bruni, *The Age of Grievance* (Avid Reader Press/Simon & Schuster, 2024), 238. Bruni's persuasive argument for media literacy and civics education in the age of AI inspired much of this prefatory essay. See especially 233–39.

Acknowledgments

Without Marjorie Mather at Broadview Press, this book would not have come to fruition. Marjorie helped me to see that an article written for history instructors could be transformed into a book that could help college students as they tackle their first historical research paper. That article was published in *The History Teacher* in 2013. Now, 12 years later, Max Uphaus, my talented and patient developmental editor at Broadview, helped me get the manuscript up to date.

All of the students I taught between 2008 and 2016—high school, college, and graduate-level—have had a hand in helping me write this book, especially those I led through the research process.

Sara Nixon helped me learn what an invaluable resource our students had in our university libraries. Dr. Ronn Pineo, Dr. Robert Rook, and Courtney Martin supported me through my creation and revision of Towson Seminars. Dr. Wayne Robertson taught me a good deal about writing instruction at the college level.

My colleagues in the Jewish History Department at Beth Tfiloh Dahan High School in Pikesville, Maryland gave me many pep talks when I struggled to balance being a teacher and an author.

I owe a huge debt of gratitude to former Beth Tfiloh students Miriam Reid ('18), Avishai Wilcox ('17), and Joshua Silber ('19), whose illustrations appear on these pages. My niece Rachel Zurier's clever cartoons in the quoting and plagiarism chapters lighten the mood in just the right way.

Dr. Paula Hyman first taught me to think and write like a historian, and the values of clarity and precision in historical argument. I wish she could be here to share this with me today.

My esteemed mentor and colleague at Brandeis University, Dr. Jonathan Sarna, has been an incredible support throughout every twist and turn of my career.

I am blessed with a terrific support network that starts with an incredibly close-knit family. My four sisters are my biggest cheerleaders when I hit roadblocks.

How I wish I could call my parents and in-laws now to share the news that this book finally became a reality. My amazing mom and dad, Irena and David Sandler, taught me how important it is to love what you do and to live with integrity. My mother- and father-in-law, Susan and Allan Thaler, were never failing in their support of my professional goals.

To my extended family—my brothers-in-law, nieces, nephews, and cousins—you have cheered me on from afar, and I am so grateful for your encouragement.

My husband, Alex Thaler, has been amazingly supportive and helpful. You share your love, creativity, and good humor every day.

To our daughter Sabrina: I dedicate this book to you. You are my daily inspiration. May you always love words, research, writing, and learning.

CHAPTER 1

Don't Panic!

Let me guess. You just started the semester and picked up this book along with the others your history instructor assigned. You have taken a glance at your syllabus and see a deadline for "research paper" looming. What's worse, it's going to count for a good percentage of your final grade for this class. And it's long—maybe as long as eight to ten pages. You've never written that much before. And this is only one of several papers that you need to write this semester. Of course this isn't the only course you're taking. Is it too late to drop the class and return this book? You consider running back to the bookstore and checking the return policy posted on the window. But the course is required of all first-year students. Or, you need to take a history course at some point. So you really don't have a choice. You need to write that paper somehow.

Keep the Big Picture in Mind

It is entirely normal to feel anxious right now as you contemplate this project. Unless you are a seasoned researcher, I would be really surprised if this project didn't make you anxious. Take some comfort in the fact that most of the students in your class probably feel the same way.

A little anxiety can help motivate you to get moving. You have already done something right in that you have noted what is likely the major assignment on your course syllabus. Now, channel that anxiety into positive, constructive energy and get started. Don't wait until the last minute.

You do not need to produce a literary masterpiece. First-year history instructors do not expect their students to write a PhD or Master's thesis. They also do not expect anything approaching a perfect history paper. At the introductory level, this would be an unfair and unreasonable expectation. Instead, instructors want their students to put reasonable effort into each part of the process, and not wait until the last minute. (You will see "avoiding the last minute" as a recurring theme in this book.) At this level of instruction, the research process is just as, if not more, important as the final paper. At each step, you will be challenged to make new connections, overcome obstacles, and be resourceful.

You will use research skills and strategies again in other classes. Many students overlook the fact that what they do in one class can help them succeed in other classes, as well as in their future careers. Even if you stumble along the way in this process (and you likely will), you will still benefit in the long run from the experience. So try to remember to look beyond the grade itself to what you're actually learning by making the effort.

How College Papers Differ from High School Papers

With these ideas in mind, let's take a look at the kind of writing you'll need to do in this course and contrast it with what you might have done in high school.

If you've written research papers in high school, or in the context of other history classes, you might have a head start. Some students I worked with had extensive experience doing research. But I have learned to take the word "experience" with a grain of salt.

"Research paper" could denote many types of writing, not all of which correspond to what your college instructor wants you to do. Here are the major characteristics of a historical research paper assigned at the university level, together with descriptions of how they likely differ from what you did in high school. Now, I am making generalizations here, so if your high school experience doesn't match up with what is described below, please excuse the discrepancies.

Description vs. argument- or thesis-driven research. Sometimes, students equate "research" with gathering facts about the past. In this sense, "research" means taking notes and assuming that what you read and write

Research Papers in High School vs. College

ELEMENT OF PAPER	HIGH SCHOOL	COLLEGE
What is "Research?"	Descriptive	Argument/thesis-driven
Style of writing	Reporting/summarizing	Critical and argument-based
Level of detail	Superficial/basic facts	Greater focus, more detail
Primary sources	May use some or none	Variety of primary sources required
Historiography	Not usually considered	Important
Scholarly sources	Recommended, perhaps not required	Required

down is accurate and should not be questioned. This might have worked in grade school, and perhaps even for some high school papers. At the college level, however, students writing historical papers don't just write down whatever they read and submit a chronology of historical facts as their history paper. In short, a college history paper is not a Wikipedia article.

Instead, students are encouraged to ask questions like "why" or "how" as they relate to the historical events they are studying. They *investigate* the past more critically, and look for sources that corroborate the data they initially found. They form their own conclusions about the past and defend them. Research at the college level calls for much more active engagement on the part of the student, as opposed to passive absorption of information.

College instructors require an *argument* or *thesis* at the heart of your research paper. Rather than just describing an event, as in an encyclopedia or other reference work, developing a thesis means that you ask a question about an event or person and try to answer it in your own way. The answer that you come up with is your argument, or *thesis*. The thesis puts forth a particular interpretation of an event or series of events, or explains the relationship among multiple events.

This difference between description and argumentation is distilled in the very word "essay" itself. I wrote just now that, in university research essays, you will be expected to "try to answer" a question about the past—and in fact the word "essay" comes from the French verb *essayer*, meaning "to try." Every essay, then, should be an attempt—an attempt to persuade your reader of the plausibility of your argument, and an attempt (to refer to the title of this book) to solve a puzzle. At the college level, you should no longer just be describing "what happened" in the past, or even just describing the solutions to a particular puzzle about the past that previous historians have put forward; instead, you should be advancing your own particular solution to a puzzle from the past and trying to convince others to accept it.

Descriptive writing vs. analytical writing. The second difference between high school- and college-level papers follows logically from the first. As you would expect, if your notion of "research" needs to shift in college, so does your definition of what "writing" means. In high school, on the one hand, you might have been able to get away with doing much less original thinking. College-level history papers, on the other hand, call for critical thinking and writing skills. In high school, if your assignments asked you to "report on" an event or "describe" an idea, chances are good that your instructor did not ask you to put forth your own interpretation or understanding of a topic. College-level history papers will require you to take a stab at making your own point about a topic.

Now, it's important to point out that *all* historical writing incorporates descriptions of events: it's impossible to write a research paper in college without first telling your reader "what happened." The difference in college-level writing is that this description is *in service of* a larger argument, while in high school the description might have been all that you were asked to do.

Focus and depth vs. superficial accounts of the past. High school papers can often cover a very broad topic in rather limited depth. As is possible with much descriptive writing, it's acceptable to write in broad strokes and make big generalizations about the past. University-level writing asks you to explore a topic in detail, much more so than you did in high school. You need to be able to take a broad topic, narrow it to a manageable size, and then research that topic in greater depth than you have in the past. Your goal in a university-level research paper is not to figure out how much of a broad topic you can cover, but to delve deeply into one specific issue and extract its riches.

My college students had questions that highlight this difference in expectations: On many occasions, they asked how I could possibly expect them to write ten pages on a particular topic, because they'd be finished writing by page five. Or, as one of my high school students asked when discussing a research topic for a five-page paper, "Why should I concentrate on a five-year time span of history? I could discuss a half-century."

Both of these questions reflect the assumption that the student's chief task is "covering ground," rather than "digging deeply."

Professional historians choose one issue and explore it from all sides, or as many sides as they can access. They look beneath the chronology presented in an encyclopedia article and ask questions of why and how. They are skeptical of their sources. Doing historical research is akin to playing the detective who tries to solve a mystery. Your instructor doesn't expect you to have the expertise or experience of a professional historian but does want you to practice using those skills when you write this paper.

Reliance on primary sources. Descriptive writing relies chiefly on secondary sources, which are produced by historians or others who are far removed from the historical period they are writing about. But college-level research papers require you to wrestle with primary sources, which are those artifacts or documents produced during the time frame you're writing about.

What's the difference? Primary sources are critical to any research paper at the college level because they represent the voices of those you're studying. You cannot formulate a thesis about a topic if you have not consulted primary sources. While the number of primary sources you're required to use will vary depending on the topic you've chosen, typically your instructor will want to see a few types of sources used, or a few perspectives represented. In other words, if you are studying the 1920s, you might consult a few magazine articles, newspaper stories, and pictures from the period. If you are studying diary entries collected from the Civil War era, you might select those from enslaved people, enslavers, and abolitionists. The precise combination of sources is up to you, but they should be documents that you actively incorporate into your research.

Attention to historiography, or the historical conversation on your topic. You don't hear too much about historiography in most high school classrooms (though there are some exceptions). In a college-level research paper, you are usually expected to have some knowledge of what other scholars have written on the topic you have chosen. Historians call this "historiography." For instance, if I'm studying some local leaders of the Civil Rights Movement, I'd want to take a look at some of the historical literature that has been written about those individuals thus far. Have any biographies been published on someone from the community on which I'm focusing? What about more general texts that can tell me a little about what else was going on in that community at the time? Is there a topic or theme that seems to be controversial among historians? If so, what side do I support?

Historiography refers not only to the conversation taking place on one topic in a particular time period, but also to the way in which that discussion has evolved *over time*. Our understandings of events change as time passes, as we gain the greater perspective afforded by chronological distance from an event. Let's return to the example of the Civil Rights leaders. As you'd expect, the way that historians wrote about them in the 1970s is far different from what was written in 2010 or is being written today. Though history itself hasn't changed, our interpretations of the past are always changing. That's why publishers update American history textbooks periodically.

Just as Gerald Graff and Cathy Birkenstein argue in *They Say/I Say*,[1] writing a college-level paper implies that you are sitting down at a table with a group of scholars, each of whom has written on your topic (or a related topic). You share your own perspective not in a vacuum, but in response to theirs. When you are capable of describing your own perspective on an event in relation to what other historians have said, you dramatically increase your credibility as a writer. Acknowledgment of others' opinions shows that you are well-versed on the scholarship (or historiography) on your topic. We will address this topic further in Chapter 9.

Use of scholarly source material. Students I taught at the college level often told me that when they wrote papers for high school classes, they could find all of their information online. They typically meant that they did a Google search and found everything they needed. (At that time, at least, the reliability of websites did not seem to be as much in question.) For college-level papers, you should start with the university's library catalog. Most of your secondary sources for a college-level history paper will be books (or e-books) that you get from your library's collection. Later, once you have a better sense of your topic and what your argument might be, you will probably be able to find some scholarly journal articles on your topic when you peruse your library's research databases.

Why do you need to retrieve books from the physical shelves, when for several years you've managed to complete everything with just a couple of Google searches? The scholars who have written on your topic express their viewpoints primarily in books published by university presses, and in journal articles that have been *peer-reviewed*. What does this mean? Unlike what you might find on websites intended for general audiences, the materials you will find in peer-reviewed sources have been vetted by scholars in

1 *They Say/I Say: The Moves That Matter in Academic Writing*, 3rd ed. (W.W. Norton, 2014).

the field for accuracy, or at least legitimacy. The review process for historical writing is very rigorous. Authors must have the appropriate academic credentials and their manuscripts are reviewed by other scholars before publication. By the time you get those items off the library shelves, they've been reviewed and edited a number of times to meet a set of strict criteria.

This isn't to say that there aren't reliable websites that come up in your Google searches. There are many. But you have to know how to find them. Virtually anyone can pose as a "historical expert" online, and the array of disinformation to be found on the internet and in social media often makes it hard to distinguish truth from fiction. When doing research at the college level, we first access the sources that have already been vetted, rather than trust ourselves to make that judgment.

With these main differences in mind (all of which will be discussed in more depth later in this book), we turn to the next chapter, where we talk about the fundamental goal of research papers in history courses and the skills you hone as a result of working on this type of project.

See Online Companion Exercises for Chapter 1
sites.broadviewpress.com/puzzle/chapter-1

CHAPTER 2

Starting Off on the Right Foot

Now that you know a bit more about the differences between papers assigned in college and high school, let's think about something else. Why in the world do you have to do this anyway? What purpose does it serve? Many of my students remarked, "Dr. Thaler, we've gotten along in life just fine up until this point without doing one of these things. So why start now?" These are entirely valid questions.

Throughout this process, what you want to keep in mind is that the more effort you put into it, the more you'll get out of it. Though you're doing a project in the context of one college course, the research paper actually requires skills that you will use in a variety of different courses and professions, well beyond the classes you are taking now.

Skills Honed by the Research Process

Writing a research paper requires sustained concentration on one problem for an extended period of time. Unless you plan to enter a profession in which you do precisely the same types of tasks every day, your future job will probably throw some curveballs your way from time to time. You're not going to have all the answers the first day you receive an assignment, and will have to stick with it for a while to figure out a solution.

Writing a research paper requires you to think critically. Since a historical paper requires you to ask questions about the past rather than simply describe events, you need to think carefully, develop arguments, and defend them with sources. You need to formulate your own logical opinions and explain why they make sense. Regardless of what profession you choose to enter, you'll likely need to be able to explain why your approach to a problem makes the most sense. You will also need to put forth evidence in defense of your perspective.

Writing a research paper requires you to evaluate the merits and shortcomings of others' arguments. When you consider other historians' perspectives on your topic, you need to determine your points of agreement and disagreement, and express your views in a respectful and clear way. That same skill is required in virtually every type of group project you'll work on in college and in your career, regardless of what it might be.

Writing a research paper requires you to prioritize information, separating what is most important from what is less relevant. Most simply put, the research process is all about making sensible choices. When you select primary sources, you need to determine which ones are most relevant to your thesis and put aside those that don't apply.

Writing a research paper requires you to develop or advance an argument. Students new to the writing of research papers often make the mistake of repeating, rather than developing, their thesis statements—the sentence or two early in your paper in which you state the paper's main argument. A thesis statement, or argument, should not remain static. It is not a mantra that repeats throughout your paper. Instead, it should develop in an incremental way throughout the paper, and become stronger and more believable as it evolves. This requires a lot of practice, and is a rhetorical skill useful in settings that rely on strategies of persuasion—law or politics, for instance.

Writing a research paper requires you to give credit where credit is due. Careful source citation is one of the less exciting aspects of writing a research paper, but it is also one of the most important. Getting in the habit of citing your sources in an organized, methodical fashion might mean the difference between a good grade and a failing grade. In a work setting, it could determine whether you come across as conscientious or sloppy. In extreme cases, proper citation practice may help you keep your job.

Writing a research paper requires you to identify main ideas and arguments in others' writing. This critical reading skill means that you know how to get to the heart of the matter, and distinguish main points from supporting details. This is a tool you use every time you open up a textbook in college or take notes on what someone says.

Writing a research paper requires you to summarize and paraphrase others' ideas fairly, without plagiarism. When you describe another writer's perspective, are you able to represent them accurately, even if you disagree with the points they are making? This skill is essential to every academic discipline where scholars or professionals review or rely upon each other's contributions. It is also necessary for group projects that build on work done previously.

Writing a research paper requires you to organize your ideas in a logical fashion. Outlining papers is one of the toughest steps of the research process—but your paper will collapse if you can't master this skill. Outlining well means that you know how to think in a step-by-step fashion that makes sense not only to you but to others. Whether you are doing an oral presentation or a grant proposal, being able to determine a clear progression of ideas is a must.

Writing research papers requires you to manage your time properly. This is not an overnight project, and you need to anticipate slip-ups and stumbles along the way. Those who do research papers at the last minute will almost inevitably come up short.

Writing research papers requires you to write clearly. Yes, writing matters. Historians tend to be very precise, careful writers who believe that writing should be accessible to general audiences. Students often asked me why I took off points for improper spelling, grammar, and other writing errors. Invariably, I explained that every course that is taught in English is an English course. Poor writing skills will hold you back in many careers, too.

See Online Companion Exercise 2A
sites.broadviewpress.com/puzzle/chapter-2

What a Research Project Is Not

Hopefully I have convinced you by now that this project is worth your effort. Just as important, though, is dispelling a few of the myths about research papers that some students have.

Research projects are a waste of time. Just put in the least effort possible and get a passing grade. Clearly, there are skills to be learned from this assignment, even if they are difficult for you to master. If there were nothing to be gained, you would not be given the assignment in the first place.

Now, students can get extremely frustrated in the course of their research. That's a natural and understandable response to a new challenge. But rather than request help and use the resources available to them, some students simply act resentful of their teacher for requiring the assignment in the first place. This is an immature and counterproductive attitude to adopt. College instructors don't design their syllabi in a vacuum. Your college or university faculty and administrators want you to learn these skills—and, as I hope the previous section has made clear, they have good reason for wanting you to do so. You need to do this assignment, and you might as well do your best.

Research papers involve cutting and pasting a bunch of web passages into one document, and changing a few words here and there in order to elude plagiarism detection software—or telling an AI platform, "Write an essay on [X topic]." Please don't make this mistake. You will get caught sooner or later. And even if you don't get caught in the course of your college career, doing this will teach you nothing and waste your time and money.

Research papers are a chance to tell professors what they want to hear, or to repeat something that they said in class. Nothing could be further from the truth. The point of the project is to give you the chance to do independent study and formulate your own conclusions. Even if your instructor disagrees with your thesis statement, what matters is whether you adequately prove it with evidence and logic.

How This Book Can Help

Research papers vary depending on the discipline in which they're assigned. Here's why this book is necessary.

A history paper is different from other kinds of papers. Many students assume that the research paper they wrote in their high school English class will prepare them for writing papers in other disciplines. It is true that a history paper has a thesis statement, a bibliography, and other elements common to expository writing. But don't confuse the common *elements* with the very different *strategies and thought processes* required to craft those elements in each discipline. The process of researching and writing a history paper requires a particular set of skills. Each discipline has its own conventions, or rules, that characterize academic writing done in that field. The reason you're asked to write papers in each topic you explore is that writing in a particular discipline helps you learn to think like a scholar in that discipline. Writing itself is a key pedagogical tool.[1]

I find it useful to think of each discipline as having its own "language." By language, I mean a set of priorities or expectations about what constitutes a decent piece of writing in that discipline. Historians speak one language, scholars of English literature speak another, anthropologists have their own, and so on. If you begin writing your historical research paper with the expectation that the finished product will look just like the English or political science paper you recently completed, you'll likely get into trouble. You will write what *you* think is a perfectly satisfactory paper, only to discover when it's too late that your instructor was looking for something quite different. You'll get comments back on your paper that you did not anticipate, and you will ultimately feel that your instructor did not evaluate your paper fairly. In part, your history instructor assigned this book in order to help you avoid having this frustrating experience. It's critically important that you familiarize yourself with the major features of a history paper before you start writing. Only then can you give yourself the best opportunity for success.

Many students get to college without having learned to write a historical research paper in high school. Up until the mid-1990s, most American high school students wrote research papers at some point in their history classes. They went to their public libraries, sifted through the card catalogs, and checked out books the old-fashioned way (with stamped due dates!). Such began the long haul called the "research process." In the last thirty to thirty-five years, however, many public high schools have done away with this rite of passage. Due to larger class sizes and competing demands on teachers' time, students today often arrive at college with little to no experience doing a full-fledged, independent research project. Those students who did have the experience of writing a research paper in high school often wrote a shorter essay, or engaged in only some aspects, but not all, of the research process. Advanced Placement history classes focus on a different writing process that calls for document analysis, but not original research.

---

1 "An Introduction to Writing across the Curriculum," posted June 14, 2011, by OWLPurdue, YouTube, 5 min., 12 sec., www.youtube.com/watch?v=RXyxLRSQsoI.

Due to this curricular shift in many high schools across North America, it now falls to colleges and universities to teach students how to write research papers, specifically in the context of first-year seminars. The traditional first-year English class has been replaced in recent years with what one scholar calls "basic training in writing expository essays and research papers."[2] At first glance, this curricular decision may seem to make good sense, but it really only works well for those who have already had at least some background doing research prior to college. While these first-year writing classes may be smaller than large lecture courses, taking on the challenge of writing a research paper is very difficult for most first-year students. They need a lot of one-on-one attention to have their individual needs addressed. The prospect of approaching a college professor during office hours is daunting to many students, so they try to manage on their own. Combine that with the other pressures of the first year of college, and it's not surprising that students don't usually master the art of research in two short months.

The steps you take to write a good history paper are not intuitive, particularly in the Age of Google. Though it may seem at first blush that writing a paper in the digital age is a piece of cake, it's actually more challenging than you might think. With so much information at your fingertips, you need to know how to sift through what's available, separate what to rely upon from what to ignore, and determine what to paraphrase, summarize, and quote. When you paraphrase, you restate an author's original ideas in your own language. To summarize, however, means to explain an author's main point concisely. When you quote, you incorporate the author's language exactly as it appears in the original text.

You need to know how to narrow a topic from a vague idea into a concise, focused research question, the frame for your project that will be discussed extensively in Chapter 5. And perhaps most challenging of all of these tasks, you need to come up with an original idea or perspective on the information you find that reflects your own thinking and creativity—an original idea that will become your paper's thesis. The process of writing a historical research paper is just that: a process. And when done properly, it's not

---

2 Peter Wood, "'It Messes Up My Fishing Time': Why American High School Teachers Don't Assign Research Papers," *National Association of Scholars* (blog), October 14, 2010, www.nas.org/blogs/article/. Wood also mentions the pioneering work of Will Fitzhugh, founder of *The Concord Review*, the only journal in the world devoted exclusively to publishing historical research papers written by secondary level students. Fitzhugh surveyed American high school teachers in 2002 and learned that almost two-thirds no longer assign longer research papers.

something that gets finished overnight. It takes a good deal of trial and error, as well as persistence in the face of adversity. You need to be able to arrive at the finish line and have adequate support along the way. This book is intended to provide that support.

You need these skills to be outlined in an engaging, accessible fashion. One of the reasons so many college and university courses have adopted the short guide to academic writing *They Say/I Say*, by Gerald Graff and Cathy Birkenstein, is because students find it useful and readable. Unfortunately, it's hard to say that about most available historical research guides, which tend to be written more for students who already have quite a bit of academic training. The students I have taught have complained that they found those texts impenetrable and promptly returned them to the bookstore at the end of the semester. I am writing this book to fill that gap. While I don't think you'll be bringing this book to the beach anytime soon, having a research guide that is easier to read makes it much more likely that you will use it consistently.

Your instructor wants you to enjoy the study of history. Have you ever had a bad experience in a class that completely turned you off taking more classes in the same subject? A negative experience completing a historical research paper can really turn a student off studying history at all. Nothing disappoints me more than when a student tells me that a teacher was unhelpful when she ran into a research obstacle, or that he gave up searching the library database because he simply couldn't find a helpful source. This book is intended to help you find a way out when you get stuck.

Work Habits Necessary for Writing a College-Level History Paper

Now that you understand some of the skills you will develop from doing this paper, as well as the ways in which this book can be a useful resource, let's turn to your end of the bargain. There are some work habits that will help to ensure that you succeed in this undertaking. What you need to realize is that you must work *against* what comes naturally to you and stretch a bit, almost as though you're exercising a new muscle group.

Time management. The number one problem students have with college research papers is that they don't get started soon enough. At the end of every semester, my students usually wrote in their self-evaluations, "I wish I hadn't waited so long to begin." Typically, you will receive a deadline that seems to be comfortably far away. But those deadlines tend to sneak up on you faster than you can imagine. University papers require a lot more work because of the type of thinking demanded of you at each stage of the process. What's more, many university instructors expect students to work independently, or provide only limited guidance along the way.

If your instructor scaffolds your assignment—or breaks it up into smaller assignments due before the final deadline—you'll likely be able to resist the temptation to procrastinate. But if not, you should make your own artificial deadlines so that you don't end up with a paper to write in too short of a time span.

Another insight from past students' mistakes: *Actually think about each step of the research process from the beginning.* Don't just go through the motions in order to check the preliminary assignments off your to-do list. I once assigned a high school research paper with several intermediate deadlines. Though students handed in the work along the way, it was easy for me to see that some of them were clearly phoning it in at first, and were not planning to put in their best effort until the end of the project timeline. They received completion grades for doing the minimum necessary to pass the requirement, but got very little out of the work they handed in. When you get feedback from your instructor on a research question or a thesis statement, or when you find out that some of your sources aren't appropriate, your job is to act on those suggestions right away, not ignore them until later. By that time, you won't remember what your instructor was even talking about!

Managing your time well doesn't necessarily mean that you should start writing as soon as possible, especially if (like many writers at every level of skill and experience!) you find actually sitting down to write to be stressful and difficult. Spending a lot of time researching, taking notes on and evaluating sources, outlining, and so forth can be a kind of "productive procrastination": it won't yield words on the page (or screen), but it will be helpful down the road when you do finally have to sit down and start writing. In other words, don't force yourself to conform to a model of productivity that doesn't work for you; rather, effective time management at the college level is about breaking up big projects and making progress on them in a way that you find natural and comfortable.

Completing a research project, in short, is like running a marathon: You need to keep a steady pace, putting in consistent effort throughout, in order to reach the finish line. What a "steady pace" actually looks like will be different for each runner—or for each researcher. For some people, just chugging along consistently works best, while others find it more effective to go a little slower at first, precisely so that they can go for broke in the final stages. Either strategy can take you to the end of the race—or, in research terms, can yield a successful final paper. You just don't want to wait until near the end of the race to start running at all!

Patience and persistence. If you are expecting your research process to be obstacle-free, you're living in dreamland. Almost by definition, research involves lots of trial and error and experimentation. Seldom does your original plan or focus stay the same throughout the process, particularly when you are dealing with a host of "unknowns." In historical research, you can't be sure what sources you'll be able to find, and if you'll find them in a reasonable time frame in order to write the paper. You might pick a topic that is too narrow, too obscure, or simply not something you find very intriguing. Almost invariably, you will have to make adjustments.

If you anticipate that at least some of these problems may come up, you won't lose your sanity when they do occur. Research is time-consuming, unpredictable, and often quite frustrating. All the same, it's extremely rewarding when you are able to work through problems and find solutions, but you need to allow yourself the ability to do so.

I remember a conversation I had with one student several years ago that perfectly illustrates what happens when students are impatient with the research process. I couldn't figure out why he had never turned in his initial list of sources. I asked him why he had fallen behind, and he answered that he couldn't find anything during his initial search in the library catalog. He had tried two search terms and neither one yielded any results, so he gave up and left the library after ten minutes. He was so accustomed to finding what he needed immediately that he had clearly not anticipated encountering any problems along the way. An email to his instructor or a librarian would have resolved this problem and enabled him to move forward on his project. But he did not want to take the time to send it.

Historical research seldom yields immediate answers, so don't expect a quick visit to Google or a database to provide you with everything you need.

Don't multitask. The research process is a cognitively demanding task, one that merits your full attention. It's time to turn off your phone and get off social media. Eliminate all other distractions when you are working on your research, even if it's just for a few minutes at a time. In the past, students have typically dismissed this advice when I mentioned it in class, insisting that they are good multitaskers and my advice doesn't apply to them. This is not true. Brain studies have shown repeatedly that we work less effectively when shifting from one task to another.[3] You will accomplish more in your research through one hour of focused attention than by going back and forth between research, two other homework assignments, and social media.

Talk it out. A lot of students who have difficulty writing often find that they can talk about their ideas much more easily than write about them. If you have trouble getting past a conceptual obstacle along the way, don't forget to try talking aloud about your ideas. Especially if you learn best by hearing information (as opposed to reading a written text, for instance), speaking about your topic can help you process the subject matter differently. Alternatively, bounce your idea or problem off your friend or a family member. Unlike research papers in some disciplines, your history paper should be something that you can talk about relatively easily with an intelligent peer. Sure, you'll need to fill her in on the historical context and facts, but once you've done that, you may be surprised at the insight you can gain from a thoughtful, candid conversation about your topic.

Use visual aids. If you are a visual learner and prefer visual symbols or flow charts to assist in representing ideas, break out the markers and paper and get started. Sometimes when you map out your ideas in pictures instead of words, you get new insights into the direction your research is taking. This strategy can be helpful at any stage of the research process. Software such as LucidChart provides the same benefit in a digital space.[4]

Be resourceful. Your college or university has resources designed to help you with your project, but they will not magically appear at the door of your dorm room. If you are having difficulty with any step of the research process and cannot seem to find an answer, you should start by consulting your instructor. Many problems can be resolved with a short email or in a conversation during office hours.

Alternatively, you should visit the reference librarian on duty in your college library. Librarians are remarkably helpful, knowledgeable individuals

---

3 See, for instance, Adam Gorlick, "Media Multitaskers Pay Mental Price, Stanford Study Shows," *Stanford News*, August 24, 2009, http://news.stanford.edu/2009/08/24/multitask-research-study-082409/; and Travis Bradberry, "Multitasking Damages Your Brain and Career, New Studies Suggest," *Forbes*, October 8, 2014, www.forbes.com/sites/travisbradberry/2014/10/08/multitasking-damages-your-brain-and-career-new-studies-suggest/#5d88566f2c16. See also Curt Steinhorst, "Phones and Focus: How to Win the Uphill Battle of Workplace Distraction," *Forbes*, September 28, 2023, www.forbes.com/sites/curtsteinhorst/2023/09/28/phones-and-focus-how-to-win-the-uphill-battle-of-workplace-distraction/.

4 LucidChart is one example among many of diagramming software available online. Others include Miro and ClickUp.

who have been trained to assist students with precisely the types of problems that they typically have when doing research. Librarians may be able to help you find appropriate books or use the library's databases more efficiently by changing your search strategies. Some college libraries also have subject specialists who work with students on certain types of papers. They will know the most about the library's holdings in your area of concentration.

Remember as well that some of your sources for a research paper might need to come from other libraries. You may find that another university library in your state or province has a much better collection of works on your topic, and that it takes a few days for those sources to make it to your own library. You may need to use services such as Interlibrary Loan, which enable you to borrow books that are owned by libraries located far from your own. Sometimes the source you need may take longer than you'd think to reach you—up to a month in some cases (though this is unusual). This is just one more reason why time management is critical in completing a research project.

Clear writing counts. Your history instructor expects you to write clearly, so please allow enough time to revise your draft. Historical writing needs to be concise and clear, as it's very easy to confuse your reader otherwise. Writing matters just as much as it would in any other course. University Writing Centers often help students with their writing at every stage of the writing process, not just when a full draft is complete. Please take advantage of this terrific resource.

See Online Companion Exercise 2B
sites.broadviewpress.com/puzzle/chapter-2

Looking Ahead to the Research Process

This book walks you through every stage of the research process. These stages are presented in the visual guide below. Chapters 3, 4, and 5 address finding a topic, narrowing it to a manageable scope, and writing a research question. This is the initial part of the project in which you'll be looking for resources, figuring out what precise topic you're interested in, and determining the question you'll answer in the course of your research. Chapters 6–10 help you to figure out how to find and analyze sources, write a thesis statement that reflects your evidence, acknowledge alternative viewpoints, and organize your ideas. Lastly, the third section of the book focuses on the writing of the paper. Chapters 11 and 12 help you to understand the conventions of history writing, as well as the key elements of a historical research paper. Chapters 13–15 cover source citation, the appropriate use of quotations, strategies for avoiding plagiarism, and using generative AI responsibly. The companion website provides some practice exercises to help you review some of the skills taught in this book. Completing these exercises should help to boost your confidence in your research skills.

It's important to remember that there are countless resources for writing excellent history papers, and it's quite likely that if you're having trouble with any part of the research process, you'll be able to find extra help online. Ultimately, your instructor should always be the first resource you turn to.

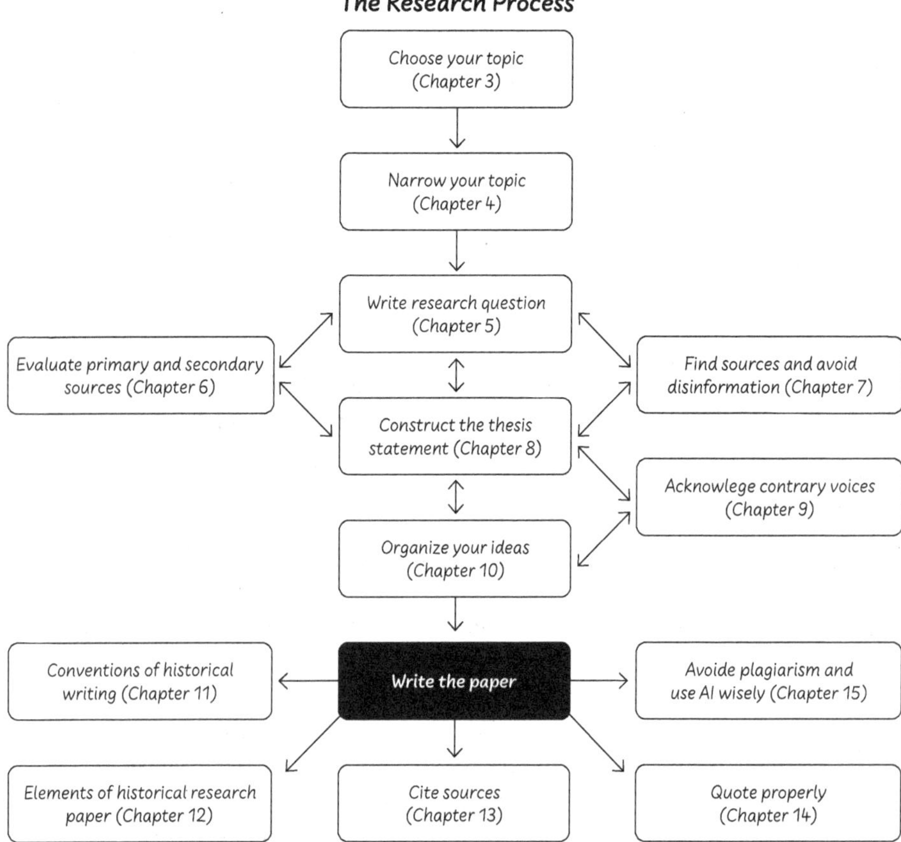

A Word of Encouragement

I have a feeling that as you near the conclusion of this chapter, you may be worried. A lot of the work habits and requirements of college-level papers probably sound pretty daunting. Maybe you did a research paper in high school that was not too difficult to complete, and for which you received an A. Perhaps the topic you started with was precisely what you'd been studying in class, and the process was entirely predictable and problem-free. Maybe your teacher helped you out by assigning the project in stages, so that you didn't have to manage your own deadlines. I hear you saying all of this—I heard it so many times from nervous students at the start of this process—and I know that you are concerned.

But you can do this. You just have to take it a little at a time. The information presented here isn't intended to scare you off, believe it or not. Rather, it's meant to provide you with a bit more insight into what this project requires. Students who stuck with me from the beginning of the process to the end did well on their final papers. Those who procrastinated often ended the semester in a very different place, usually asking themselves why they hadn't worked harder early on.

With an open mind and willingness to endure some trial and error—and ask lots of questions when you need help—you might actually find the process of discovery to be fun at times. I know what you're thinking: *Fun?* Seriously? My response: Yes! This book takes its name from the thought process that is required to solve a mystery, or a puzzle. The puzzle metaphor, in fact, is one that many professional historians use to describe their work and explain what drew them to it and why they enjoy doing it. One 2016 study of PhD candidates in university history programs, for example, found that seven out of ten of them "drew an analogy between writing history and fitting together the pieces of a difficult jigsaw puzzle." As one participant in the study put it, "the whole project [of writing history] is a bunch of puzzle pieces that are all locking together"; in another's words, "the most exciting thing about history is you're solving very complicated puzzles all of the time."[5] History, as studied and practiced at the college level, *is* puzzling—a process of creation, interpretation, problem-solving, and discovery, rather than just the memorization of facts, names, and dates.

---

5 Jack Schneider and Sivan Zakai, "A Rigorous Dialectic: Writing and Thinking in History," *Teachers College Record* 118, no. 1 (2016), www.holycross.edu/sites/default/files/files/education/a_rigorous_dialectic.pdf.

Throughout the semester, or whatever number of weeks you'll be engaged in research and writing, you'll be putting the puzzle together. And there's no greater satisfaction than inserting that final piece.

CHAPTER 3

Choosing the Topic

"Choose a topic for your research paper." It sounds easy enough. How hard could that be? Just as a writer can feel overwhelmed at the sight of a blank screen on her computer, students often complained about staring into the "topic abyss," feeling completely lost. They had absolutely no idea of how to start. Accustomed to receiving a discrete set of instructions for what to do to meet an assignment's objectives, students often panicked when they realized that an independent research project is, in some respects, open-ended. I had students plead with me to suggest a topic so that they could avoid having to make the decision for themselves. The problem with this approach was that I was not writing the paper. If I did provide a suggestion, the student usually responded, "Can you come up with something else? I don't find that very interesting."

For an independent research project, you get to set your own agenda. It's possible that some instructors may provide you with some guidelines for what is acceptable, or even a list of potential topics from which to choose. The "blank screen" response you might have, though, is a normal reaction to receiving a new type of assignment. I can promise you that most people in your class probably feel the same way you do. That said, I strongly encourage you to work through the discomfort so that you can find a topic that you will enjoy studying.

What to Do When You Get the Assignment

Read the assignment provided by your instructor, and get your questions answered. It may sound obvious, but students frequently ignore this most basic source of information. Read all of the instructions your teacher has provided, whether they are on the syllabus you received at the start of the course or on a separate handout. Save all of the materials you receive. Approach your teacher in person or via email with any questions you may have at this point.

Visit your college or university library to see if your instructor has provided other materials to help you start your project. Your professor may work closely with reference librarians to help provide you with introductory sources. These may include online or print encyclopedias owned by your library, or a list of the most appropriate commercial databases for the area of history you are focusing on.

Get to know your university's reference librarians. Don't be shy. Your reference librarian's job is to assist students with research projects. Students often neglect to speak to their librarians until the last minute, and then get frustrated when the librarian does not have adequate time to respond to their requests for help.

Mark down your deadlines on your academic calendar. If you have received a set of deadlines for separate stages of the project, then write them down right away and start planning accordingly. If not, you should make your own schedule for completing this paper so that you can pace yourself and are not tempted to procrastinate.

See Online Companion Exercise 3A
sites.broadviewpress.com/puzzle/chapter-3

Suggestions for Finding a Topic that Interests You

Brainstorm topics or themes of your history course thus far that you have found most intriguing or engaging. Have you asked questions in class recently about something in particular? Have you jotted notes in the margins of your textbook that reflect your skepticism, strong disagreement, or pronounced interest in something that you read?

Think about the events, struggles, or causes that have fueled your passion to learn, and explore their historical roots. Many students find historical topics particularly engaging when they are able to relate them to something that is already part of their own world. Here are some examples from classes I taught:

- One student who felt strongly about eco-friendly behaviors researched the origins of the environmental movement. She studied Rachel Carson's classic book *Silent Spring* and its popular reception in 1962.
- One student who was troubled by America's ongoing engagement in the Iraq War in 2010–12 noticed that pundits at the time were frequently comparing it to the Vietnam War. He questioned the accuracy of those comparisons, so he decided to study the debate over the US presence in Vietnam between 1965 and 1968.
- One student who loved Broadway musicals wanted to figure out how they had evolved over time, so she compared an older musical with one from a later period.
- One student's parents grew up in the 1960s and were formerly hippies. Today, like many Baby Boomers, they romanticized Haight-Ashbury (the San Francisco neighborhood associated with the rise of the hippie movement). He decided to research the way Haight-Ashbury residents felt about the "hippie invasion" when it actually occurred in 1967.
- One student from a military family was curious about the American public's perception of the military at various times in US history. She investigated the way American veterans were treated after their return from Vietnam.
- One student whose grandmother was a child survivor of the Holocaust decided to explore efforts to rescue young people from Nazi Germany in the 1930s.
- One student completing a degree in journalism studied news anchors of the 1960s, such as Walter Cronkite, and public perceptions of them at the time.
- One student interested in contemporary gender dynamics researched print magazine advertisements for cigarettes in the 1960s, with a focus on their very different portrayals of men and women.

Follow the news. Sometimes the best research topics can come from contemporary news events. Just as your own personal history might lead you to explore particular areas of the past that would have been unknown to you otherwise, current news stories provide an unending source of material for further study. Reflecting on events that have recently taken place at the time of this book's publication, here are some examples of what comes to mind.

- Rising authoritarianism and threats to democracy.

In the last decade, democratic institutions and forms of government around the world have come under threat. Established authoritarian states have become increasingly assertive and expansionist—as seen, for example, in Russia's 2022 invasion of democratic Ukraine—while in countries such as Brazil, Hungary, the Philippines, and India (to name a few), populist leaders who in most cases gained power by democratic means have steadily eroded key democratic institutions, including free elections and an independent media and judiciary, and concentrated power in their own hands. In the United States, meanwhile, intense political polarization and widespread loss of faith in the political process on the part of much of the population have caused what many observers have characterized as a crisis of democracy—a crisis that was both exploited and intensified by the first presidency of Donald Trump. In his first term, Trump repeatedly demonstrated contempt for democratic institutions and norms. Encouraged and abetted by the former president, Trump's supporters disrupted the peaceful transfer of power by storming the US Capitol on January 6, 2021, seeking to prevent the certification of Joe Biden's victory in the 2020 presidential election.

At the time of this writing, Trump has won the 2024 presidential election, defeating Vice President Kamala Harris. Unlike in 2016, he won the popular vote as well as the electoral college, performing better across most demographics than he did in 2016 and 2020. Pundits will spend the next decades debating the reasons for Trump's ascendancy in American politics; most acknowledge the threat to American democracy that he embodies.

Numerous commentators have drawn comparisons between the present-day crisis of democracy, in the US and around the world, and previous moments in history in which democratic or republican forms of government came under threat or succumbed to authoritarianism. The takeover of Germany by Hitler and the Nazis is one frequently noted comparison, as are other examples from Europe in the 1930s. The Nazis were also brought to power by democratic means after a prolonged period in which Germany's political divisions became deeper and more bitter, and its democratic institutions weakened. US history contains many examples of political figures who have been characterized as authoritarian (such as Huey P. Long in Louisiana in the 1920s and 1930s) and of the subversion or overthrow of democratic governments (such as in Wilmington, North Carolina, in 1898). Much further back in history, the Roman Republic's transformation into the Roman Empire is another famous example of the downfall of a kind of democracy (although the Roman Republic was hardly democratic by today's standards).

When exploring such prior historical instances of rising authoritarianism and democratic crisis, resist the temptation to make facile comparisons between the present and the past. For instance, any comparison with the rise to power of the Nazis in Germany is complicated by the fact that, when the Nazis took over, Germany had only been a democracy for a little over a decade. Remember that we don't yet have much chronological perspective on what is taking place in our current political climate. Instead, use the current political drama to get ideas of what might interest you historically.

- The fraught relationships between police and citizens of color.

The last decade has witnessed cities engulfed by anguish, protest, and violence over what many people believe to be racial profiling of African Americans—in particular, their unjustified or unprovoked killing by the police. We could list any number of cities wrestling with the problems that result when civilians feel that law enforcement officers are at best indifferent—and at worst actively hostile—to the African American citizens that these officers are theoretically sworn to protect. The Black Lives Matter Movement formed in response to what many believe to be deep-seated inequities within American society. For your research project, you may want to explore the historical roots of this problem. One approach might be to investigate the relationship between race and racism, policing, and civil unrest in another period of history.

When looking for perspective on the widespread protests of recent years, members of the media typically mention the 1960s. Racial, economic, and political tensions in the United States reached a pinnacle in that decade, as large numbers of African Americans resisted segregation through concerted campaigns of civil disobedience, to which white police forces frequently responded violently. Later in the decade, unrest spiked again when a broadly unpopular war in Vietnam caused the drafting of Black men in disproportionately high numbers. The news media broadcast the resultant conflicts on television for the very first time. But this is where your job as a historian gets the most interesting: As you search the past for precedents, think carefully and resist easy conclusions. What made the 1960s similar to, and different from, the 2010s and 2020s? Historians don't just accept easy comparisons between one decade and another; they challenge the assumptions that lie beneath the surface. What factors caused today's social unrest? How are those factors similar to, and different from, what occurred in the 1960s? How did the situation evolve in various regions of the country, and why?

- Attitudes toward immigrants and immigration.

We've all heard the statement "America is a nation of immigrants." But even if immigration is central to the nation's self-definition and most cherished national values, attitudes and policies toward immigrants have varied widely over the course of our history. In the 2024 American political cycle, falsehoods pertaining to some immigrants grew so widespread on social media that some immigrant groups feared for their safety. Rumors of higher crime rates in the immigrant community had no basis in fact, nor did the claim that the American housing shortage is a result of higher levels of immigration.[1] Right-wing leaders encouraged voters to fear and suspect immigrants, whether legal or illegal.[2] Following Trump's general election win, his political opponents, as well as the US military, nervously anticipated his attempts to order the mass deportation of the country's undocumented immigrants.

In the light of these current events, you may choose to research how historical context has contributed to US government policy toward immigrants, or to social views or attitudes toward immigrants. Typically, periods of economic stress and dislocation have contributed to the United States closing its doors to immigrants in need. During the Great Depression, some immigrants found themselves the targets of considerable prejudice and

1 See Michael C. Bender, "On the Trail, Trump and Vance Sharpen a Nativist, Anti-immigrant Tone," *New York Times*, September 22, 2024. See also National Institute of Justice, "Undocumented Immigrant Offending Rate Lower Than U.S.-Born Citizen Rate," September 12, 2024, https://nij.ojp.gov/topics/articles/undocumented-immigrant-offending-rate-lower-us-born-citizen-rate.

2 See Sabrina Rodriguez, "Trump Amplifies Falsehoods about Immigrants in Closing Appeal," *Washington Post*, October 11, 2024.

discrimination, perhaps most notably Mexican Americans. During World War II, conflict with Japan resulted in oppressive measures taken against American citizens of Japanese origin.

Again with current events in mind vis-à-vis immigration, investigate how these issues played out in another era of American history. What issue made Americans anxious in your chosen period, and how were immigrants affected by those attitudes? Did some groups of immigrants fare better than others? If so, why? Were you to study the same set of issues in other countries, try to establish the relationship between immigration and national identity that exists or has existed in that country and the place that immigrants occupied in its history.

See Online Companion Exercise 3B
sites.broadviewpress.com/puzzle/chapter-3

What Makes a Topic a "Good Choice"?

What makes a topic a good choice for a historical research paper? Try to find something that ultimately meets all of the following requirements.

The topic should be something you have not studied extensively already. If you decide to study a topic that you already know a great deal about, you will find it difficult to approach it except from the perspective that you know best. One key objective of a research paper is to view or analyze a topic from multiple angles.

I once had a college student write a paper on a classic rock band that he had been a fan of for years. This seemed like a great idea to him. He figured he would be able to save a trip to the library by using the books he already owned. The problem was that those books were not appropriate sources for a research paper. He also had trouble getting enough distance from the topic to determine how he could write about the band more objectively, as opposed to from a fan's perspective. This approach might have been appropriate had he been asked to write a review of a new album, but it did not make much sense for a research paper.

Another type of problem that might come up if you choose a topic that you are already familiar with is academic integrity. If you have written a paper on the same topic in a previous class, writing about it again is a foolish idea, because a professor could think you are trying to get out of doing the work required for this project. Submitting the same paper (or even a similar paper) for two different college courses is an academic integrity violation. You need to complete your research for this topic during the semester in which it was assigned.

Keep in mind, as well, that it is incredibly easy for your instructor to figure out that you're writing about a topic that you already have written on once before. Students frequently forget that tools such as Turnitin.com, and other plagiarism checking software, retain copies of every paper submitted. It is always better to write on a new topic in order to avoid any potential trouble.

The topic should be something that you want to think about for a while. This may sound obvious, but very frequently students underestimate the amount of time it takes to do a research paper, and choose something that only mildly interests them. They quickly realize that the topic may only interest them on a superficial level, and then end up selecting something else. That approach can result in a lot of lost time.

Remember as well that your job as a writer is to make your reader interested in your topic. If you find your topic boring after just a couple of days of reading about it, it will be very difficult to convey a different message in the course of writing a research paper.

The topic should be something that you can situate in a particular historical context. When you are about to tell a story, you first need to establish the setting in which the story takes place. When you write a history paper, you need to do the same thing. While you might not get to this point right away in your research, eventually you need a topic that you can easily contextualize, or put in the proper historical framework.

The topic you choose should be something written about by others. Make sure that the topic you select is something about which you can find information. If it is very obscure, chances are you will have a hard time accessing the sources necessary to write a good paper. By "sources," historians refer to both *primary* and *secondary* sources, both of which we will discuss in much more depth in Chapter 6. Here is a very brief overview:

- A primary source comes from the period that you are studying. For instance, if you are writing on the 1960s, you may consult some of the following:
  - speeches
  - newspaper articles

- newsreel footage
- photographs
- diary entries
- political cartoons
- magazine advertisements
- television commercials

- A secondary source describes the period you are studying from a more distant perspective. Usually, when historians refer to secondary sources, they are primarily talking about journal articles or books written by experts in the field. You can find reliable sources from an internet search, but only if you can vouch for the author's credentials. Typically, you should verify that the author of an online source (that is, not from a peer-reviewed journal) has at least a master's degree, or preferably a PhD, in history or a related field.

One more point is worth mentioning here. The secondary sources you use should reflect some historical perspective on the event that you are studying. A good rule of thumb is to make sure that there is at least a generation (20 to 30 years) between when your event took place and when your secondary source was published. Simply put, our understanding of an event changes as time passes. Historical perspective evolves. Were someone to have written a paper on the Vietnam War in 1978, just five years after American troops pulled out, it would look pretty different from something written in 2018, forty years later.

See Online Companion Exercise 3C
sites.broadviewpress.com/puzzle/chapter-3

Steps to Take Once You Have Selected a General Topic

Start reading background sources. When you find a general topic, start by looking it up in encyclopedias and historical dictionaries, as well as other online reference guides (these are called *tertiary sources*). Your job is to learn as much about your topic as possible so that you can figure out which aspect of it interests you most. This is the time when you want to be a sponge, absorbing as much background information as possible. Your reference librarian should be able to direct you to specific encyclopedias (or relevant online encyclopedia-style databases) that can help you get started.

Take notes on relevant people, places, and events. Start jotting down facts about your topic so you remember the basic information that you are reading. You may want to highlight names of significant people, dates, or terms that come up frequently, because these might eventually be search terms for finding information in your library's databases or online catalog.

Write down any sources, primary and secondary, cited at the end of the articles. Typically, authors of encyclopedia articles list sources at the end of their entries that are intended to help readers find more information. These could be very helpful suggestions to you as you narrow your research focus.

Remember to take notes carefully. Even at this early stage, it is imperative that you write down every source you consult as you go. To avoid plagiarism, put quotation marks around any passage that you write down word for word. Include page numbers when you are taking notes or relevant URLs so that you don't struggle later on to figure out where you found your information.

Start asking questions about what you learn. As you read, really think carefully about what interests you about this topic. Remember that at this early stage, you may not know yet what your research focus will be. So jot down anything that comes to mind, and highlight the avenues you wish to pursue.

CHAPTER 4

Narrowing a Topic

Once you have a broad topic to consider for your project, you will need to narrow it considerably so that it is of a scope more appropriate for a short research paper. This chapter reviews the ways historians apply questions to their topics that are typically associated with basic journalism: Who, What, When, Where, Why, and How. When thinking in terms of historical research, you want to accomplish two primary objectives when asking these questions: 1) gather the relevant facts about your research topic, and 2) begin asking additional questions about the topic that may not be easily answered with tertiary sources. One of these will likely lead you to your actual research question (the topic of Chapter 5).

The deeper thinking you will do at this early stage of the research process should help you to appreciate a few of the differences between research in high school and in college. In the kind of research projects you will be assigned in college history courses, we move beyond describing what happened to asking thoughtful questions that don't have obvious answers. We also tend to prefer more focused topics over general topics, as focused topics help us to explore history in greater depth.

Questions to Ask of a Topic

Who refers to the person or group of people you are interested in studying. Who were the main actors or figures in the period? Did they do something extraordinary? Or was one person the catalyst in starting a group that was of major consequence? This is the time to go back to the notes that you took when reading your tertiary sources and see which names keep coming up repeatedly.

Remember that *who* can refer not only to the most famous individuals, but to those who assisted behind the scenes. *Who* can refer to those in charge, but also to ordinary people. You can study people who were active locally or nationally, as well as those who have not gotten much recognition.

What refers to the event or activity that took place, or to a controversy you find intriguing. List as many details as you can when answering this question, making sure you get the chronology right. Think about related *what* questions, such as, "What were the short-term and long-term consequences of this event?"

If you are dealing with a major event in history, such as a war or a social movement, remember that you're going to need to think in terms of battles or particular achievements. You can't discuss an entire war in any depth in the span of a short research paper. Again, go back to your background notes to see what you can glean from them.

For future reference, see if your event is referred to by multiple names. For instance, if you are studying a riot in the 1960s, is it called a "protest" or a "disturbance"? Was the Civil Rights Movement called the "Civil Rights Movement" at the time, or only later? Sometimes these distinctions make a big difference when you are looking for sources in your library's electronic databases or the online catalog. It can mean the difference between a satisfying search that yields helpful results and a very frustrating experience.

When, of course, refers to dates and times. Be as specific as you can, particularly if you are dealing with an event about which the dates are widely known. Chronology is extremely important to historians, but students often get sloppy and use overly vague language. Consider it a red flag if there are no dates anywhere in your notes.

If you are dealing with a complex event that took place on one day or over several days, you should have a more specific timeline that breaks days down into hours. If, for instance, you were studying a riot in the 1960s, you might first mention the event or incident that is associated with the riot most directly. Then, list the date and time of the riot, and the time at which the police responded. If people were arrested, make note of the time of the first arrest. If federal authorities were invited to the scene, indicate when that happened. Lastly, note when the tension finally dissipated.

More broadly speaking, *when* is asking you to think about the larger time period in which your event took place. When doing historical research, you need to have a pretty good idea of what people were talking about at the time. What were the hot-button issues? If you were to travel back in time to the period you're studying and pick up a copy of a daily newspaper, what sorts of stories would you find?

Often, students make the mistake of thinking that they can talk about their topic in a vacuum, steering clear of all the other events going on at the time. But remember that your characters acted in a particular historical context. If I were studying a particular urban riot in the 1960s, it would also be important for me to have in the back of my mind that these disturbances were relatively commonplace at that time.

Remember as well that *when* defines what people could have known about at the time. The historical figures you are studying could not have known what would happen the following decade, or several decades later. For that matter, they couldn't have known what would happen the very next day. Students frequently forget this when writing research papers, and write about their subject matter chiefly from a present-day perspective. Historians call this *presentism*. Now, of course we do know what happened immediately afterwards. But that doesn't give us the right to judge historical actors as if they should have known, too. The most careful researchers make a concerted effort to put themselves in the shoes of those they are studying and avoid the mistake of presentism as best they can. Taking explicit notes on when events took place will help you avoid this very common error.

Where did it take place? In what region did your event happen? If *when* asks you to think about your event in a chronological framework, *where* refers to the geographical space. Think about the part of the world you're talking about, whether it's a country, state, city, town, or neighborhood. What was that region like at the time? Did people enjoy economic stability, or was poverty a problem? Did people have jobs? Which industries were predominant? How did different races fare in the region?

Geography matters a great deal when you study political history, in particular. In the United States, the fates of political parties tend to be linked closely to region; a handful of states are even referred to as "battlegrounds" because they are less predictable than others in terms of the political party they will support in an election. Studies of race relations also must take the factor of region into consideration.

Why did this happen? The question of *why* is a bit more complicated than the other questions we've asked of our topic thus far. As the questions about your topic become more complex, you'll be relying on secondary sources to make hypotheses, some of which may contradict one another. The reason for this is that historians frequently debate *why* questions. Among other things, they may argue for the greater importance of one factor over another.

Let's think in terms of a few paths your *why* answer could take:

- *Why did an event happen?* Usually, historians argue for *multiple causality*. In other words, more than one factor is at play in understanding why any particular event took place. In the case of the Civil Rights Movement, we might argue for the influence of particular leaders at the national level, grassroots support, activist institutions, and the role of the media. We might even add the role that African American soldiers played in World War II. They questioned the values of a nation that promoted democracy abroad but did not give equal rights to its citizens at home. If we are investigating why the Civil Rights Movement took place, we need to take all these factors (and more) into account—although the relative weight or significance we assign to particular factors is a matter of interpretation and debate.
- *Why did a person act in a particular way?* When studying the decisions made by an individual, you have a slightly different type of investigation. In a sense, it is much narrower in scope. Your focus needs to be chiefly on a particular person's biography, including moments at which that individual took risks or pursued an unexpected path. Remember that refusal to act is also a decision. Bystanders are sometimes considered complicit in the unsavory acts committed by guilty parties.

  Individual stories are also challenging for historians because of the question of intention. Do you have evidence of why the person or people you are studying did what they did? Look for sources such as diary entries, correspondence, or public speeches. If no such sources exist, then historians will have to draw their own conclusions based on other primary sources from the period that shed light on the issue of motivation, as well as on other historians' arguments.

- *Why did a country or nation act in a particular way?* National leaders make decisions for a number of reasons. First of all, within one leader's administration, you may find multiple, and often competing, political views, some with more influence than others. Leaders may be up for reelection and may be trying to appeal to potential voters, which may affect policy decisions. A particular country's standing in the world, and the fears or ambitions of particular leaders or constituencies within the country regarding that standing, also plays a highly significant role in national decision-making.

How did this happen? Again, multiple causality comes into play when we try to account for a particular event or set of events. The question of *how* asks you to think about the conditions that made an event possible, or made it likely that an individual would act in a particular way. As with the *why* category, you will find that historians debate *how* questions quite frequently, arguing the relative significance of some factors over others.

Perhaps most importantly, the question of *how* requires you to think about the cultural and social contexts in which an event took place. Once again, let's take the familiar example of the Civil Rights Movement. We might say that while Martin Luther King, Jr. led the movement, he needed the backing of local activists in cities across the nation. The broadcasting of anti-Black violence and repression on television drew the attention of the nation, including its political leaders. The work of photographers caused the violence to be something that Americans saw in their newspapers and magazines on a daily basis. Institutions contributed as well, particularly Black churches committed to fighting for racial equality. Grassroots organizers made it possible for the dream of one person to become the objective that whole communities came to embrace. White northerners went south to take part in activism on behalf of their fellow Americans. Knowing all of this, how do we assess which factors were most significant to the movement's success?

To best answer the question of *how*, put yourself in the shoes of your historical actors and answer the question, "What would have been necessary for this event to happen?" Then start to brainstorm. A protest movement needs leadership and followers; it needs people going door to door to spread the word. Someone has to make posters and leaflets. Ads need to be placed in local newspapers. It needs support from at least some high-level officials to allow street demonstrations to be held, and representatives willing to cooperate with law enforcement to grant some protection for activists while they are marching. Photographers might be needed to document the event. Someone needs to raise money for all of this to take place. And the list goes on. When you brainstorm in this way, you are able to come up with questions that may be potentially rich opportunities for further investigation.

From General Topic to Narrowed Topic

Below are examples of what a student might write when first starting to take notes on two different historical topics: the early Women's Rights Movement and the Freedom Rides of the Civil Rights Movement. Both sets of notes contain a mix of facts and questions, leading to many potential directions for investigation. In terms of the early Women's Rights Movement, if I did not know much about what else was happening in American history in the 1830s to 1860s (including, of course, slavery, abolitionism, and the Civil War), I would want to add to these notes to provide myself with more context wherever I needed it. For the Freedom Rides example, I might need to become more familiar with the initial Freedom Rides conducted in 1947 so that I had a better understanding of the historical context in which the 1961 events took place. Depending on a student's background knowledge, notes on a topic could vary quite dramatically from one person to the next.[1]

1 The material for the summary of notes on the early Women's Rights Movement came from National Park Service, "Antislavery Connection," February 26, 2015, https://www.nps.gov/wori/learn/historyculture/antislavery-connection.htm#, and Town of Seneca Falls, "History of Seneca Falls," accessed March 15, 2025, senecafalls.com. The material for the summary of notes on the Freedom Riders came from Martin Luther King, Jr. and the Global Freedom Struggle, "Freedom Rides," *King Institute Encyclopedia*, https://kinginstitute.stanford.edu/.

Early Women's Rights Movement, 1830s–1870 — Notes

Who?

- Elizabeth C. Stanton (1815–1902)
- Lucretia Mott (1793–1880)
- Susan B. Anthony (1820–1906)

What?

- Lucretia Mott & others formed American Anti-Slavery Society (AASS)
- Seneca Falls Convention & Declaration of Sentiments signed
- Campaign for women's rights fueled by anti-slavery advocacy
- Formation of National Woman's Loyal League (NWLL) & support for 13th Amendment to end slavery

When?

- 1833 – Mott & others formed AASS
- 1838–40 – AASS divided into three sub-groups; AASS remained committed to women's rights
- July 19–20, 1848 – Seneca Falls Convention & Declaration of Sentiments
- 1850s – Women's state & national conventions took place across United States
- 1861 – Civil War began; state & national conventions stopped meeting
- 1863 – NWLL formed
- 1865 – Civil War ended; 13th Amendment passed
- 1870 – 15th Amendment passed (giving African American men voting rights)
- Post-1870 – Women's rights movement lost steam

Where?

- Seneca Falls, NY – known for social & religious reform
- Wesleyan Chapel (site of Seneca Falls convention)
- New York as site of NWLL support for 13th Amendment in 1864

Why?

- Why did the AASS divide in 1838–40?
- Why did anti-slavery thinking contribute to the growth of the early women's rights movement?
- Why did the NWLL turn its attention to the 13th Amendment in 1864?

How?

- How did women's state and local conventions in 1850s fuel the movement's growth?
- How did the Civil War both help and hinder early women's rights coalitions?

The Freedom Riders of the Civil Rights Movement — Notes

Who?

- Congress of Racial Equality (CORE) activists: James Farmer (1920–1999); 2. Diane Nash (1938–); 3. John Lewis (1940–2020)
- Birmingham Police Commissioner: Eugene "Bull" Connor (1897–1973)

What?

- Mixed-race bus rides, Washington, DC to Jackson, MS
- Riders fought segregation on buses traveling across state lines & at bus terminals
- In Deep South, Freedom Riders faced opposition & media covered it
- Kennedy administration got involved
- Interstate Commerce Commission (ICC) eventually prohibited segregation in interstate buses & terminals

When?

- In 1947, CORE & Fellowship of Reconciliation (FOR) set up a ride called the Journey of Reconciliation
- May 4, 1961, CORE started Freedom Rides
- On May 29, 1961, Kennedy told ICC to ban segregation in buses & facilities
- Rides went on in the summer 1961; participation grew
- On November 1, 1961, ICC put the ruling into effect; rides ended

Where?

- 1947 – CORE & FOR targeted upper South (less conflict, not too much press coverage)
- 1961 – Freedom Rides went to Deep South (more dangerous region)
- Violence in Rock Hill, SC; Anniston, AL; Birmingham, AL

Why?

- Why did student participation in the Freedom Rides increase after May 29, 1961?
- Why did violence against Freedom Riders continue?
- Why didn't MLK join a Freedom Ride?

How?

- How was media coverage influenced by the growing participation of students?
- How did the Freedom Riders feel toward MLK?
- How did media coverage influence the federal government's approach to the issue?

Try to gather similar notes for the topic that you are exploring. You might use a simple list format as depicted here, or you might draw a large visual map. For examples of "mind maps" that can be extremely helpful when brainstorming, see software such as LucidChart, ClickUp, Miro, Ayoa, or Canva. *Use whatever method you are most comfortable with, as long as you remember to consider all six questions as they pertain to your topic, and start to see your topic in terms of the questions it raises rather than just the facts associated with it.* If you've done your work properly, you will probably have more than a dozen different potential research topics listed, all of which were derived from your initial search term.

Your goal now is to focus on the aspects of the topic that you find the most intriguing. Using a highlighter, mark up whatever details you wish to explore further. This is how you slowly start to move from a general topic to a narrow topic, and eventually (in Chapter 5) to a research question.

See Online Companion Exercise 4A
sites.broadviewpress.com/puzzle/chapter-4

How do you know when you have narrowed your topic sufficiently? That's something that will be determined over time, particularly after you have framed your topic as a research question. In the meantime, here are some additional questions to ask of the potential avenues you're considering, each of which might help you to narrow your focus a bit more:

Are there enough sources available on your topic? Did you choose an aspect of your topic that can be researched easily? If you have highlighted a person's name and have seen that name multiple times, chances are this might be a safe choice. If you saw a person mentioned only once in a footnote, you might be making your job too difficult.

A related issue: If there are a slew of sources available on a historical figure (e.g., Martin Luther King, Jr.), you'll need to narrow your topic much, much further. Students who choose very popular, familiar historical figures may need to work a bit harder to get beyond what they already know.

Is your chronological period reasonable? The more sources that are available to you on a particular topic, the shorter your chronological period should be. In other words, a paper on the Civil War should probably not include more than a couple of battles, unless it's a very long paper. If, on the other hand, you are studying someone's life story and have only one source relating to your subject's childhood years, it is possible that you could cover a broader time span.

Are you able to confine your study to a particular geographical region? Students often forget that different regions experience an event in very different ways. Particularly in shorter papers, it's a good idea to concentrate on a limited geographical area so that you are not setting yourself up for overly broad conclusions. Alternatively, you might consider contrasting two regions' experiences of the same event.

What perspective(s) are you considering? Just as region is critically important, so is vantage point. Are you interested in victims or perpetrators? Are you focused instead on bystanders? The media? You can't choose everything, so try to start with two or three and narrow things from there.

See Online Companion Exercise 4B
sites.broadviewpress.com/puzzle/chapter-4

The goal of the next chapter is to write your research question: to take the aspect of your topic that you are most interested in and use it to create the frame for your puzzle. Creating your research question will help you to narrow your focus so that you have a specific strategy for going forward with your project.

I need to offer one final warning if you are already trying to cut corners and skip some steps of this process: do not choose an overly broad topic. Broad topics will leave you swimming in a sea of facts and sources with no lifeboat! Practice describing what interests you to a friend. If you can't explain it clearly, or if it sounds overly vague when you hear yourself speak, go back to the drawing board.

I hear what you're saying: "Why can't I figure this out later?" Trust me: you'll kick yourself if you don't stick to this process. You will end up with a jumble of topics and no coherent focus, and this will become abundantly clear to your professor when they have no idea what you're talking about in the first paragraph of your paper. So take my advice: follow the steps in order!

CHAPTER 5

Writing a Research Question

Now that you are familiar with your topic and understand a bit more of its complexity, you should have a better idea of why it needed to be narrowed in the first place. To say "I'm writing on the Civil Rights Movement" or even "I'm studying Martin Luther King, Jr." is not all that meaningful at the university level. As prospective research projects, both of these are far too broad.

Also, remember that your goal is to do some original thinking during the course of this project. When students start out by saying "I'm studying the Civil Rights Movement" and don't narrow their topic beyond that point, they end up with an encyclopedia article that simply lists facts and figures about this eventful period in American history. They will almost certainly have no thesis or original argument in their final paper. If you've seen the words "vague" or "too general" scrawled in the margins of past research papers, it was likely because they lacked a focused topic.

From Topic to Question

In the last chapter, we discussed the relevance of *how* and *why* questions in historical research, which help us explore issues that historians debate. You will now go back to the notes you have taken on your topic and evaluate the facts and questions you compiled. One of these will form the basis of your research question. The research question is the problem that you are trying to solve in the course of your investigation, simply framed as a question that needs to be answered. Keep this question in the forefront of your mind.

I also have come to think of the research question—to return to this book's central metaphor for historical research—as the frame for the puzzle that you're putting together. When assembling jigsaw puzzles, you typically start with the frame and then fill in the middle pieces. Constructing the frame allows you to see how everything else fits together. For a research project, the research question will help you determine what belongs in your project (your puzzle) and what you should leave out. Without a research question in place, you'll wander aimlessly through the stacks of the university library, wondering which books to pull off the shelves. You'll page through dozens of search results from commercial databases, unable to determine which articles to read and which to ignore. And perhaps most importantly, in the end you'll be unable to craft a thesis statement.

Some students get the research question and thesis statement confused. Let's get it straight from the start: the *answer* to your research question is the thesis statement. In my experience, students get confused because they were not accustomed to finding a research question in previous assignments, and instead felt they had to figure out their thesis statements immediately. Historians consider this approach backwards: they start with questions that frame their study. A historical research paper is, first and foremost, an investigation. You start an investigation with a question, not an answer.

Don't get me wrong. I'm not saying that you can't try out a potential argument for your paper. Maybe you have a theory of what your evidence will suggest, and think you know what your thesis will be in the end. That's okay. But keep in mind that this is at best a working thesis, which means that it will likely change when you collect your sources and start to learn about your topic in more detail.

Some students I've taught have been decidedly uncomfortable with this approach. They insisted on submitting their thesis statement at the start of the research process. They were so accustomed in the past to being laser-focused on the thesis that they balked when asked to try a different approach. You need to have faith that your thesis will develop in time, and it will make a lot more sense if it evolves naturally from thinking carefully about the research question.

Creating a research question is hard work, and it will take you a few tries. It's a sentence you'll revise based on how efficiently it's functioning for you as an investigative tool. Remember, its ultimate purpose is to help you arrive at your thesis statement. Typically, once students understand the purpose of the research question, they revise it numerous times in accordance with the sources they are finding. If the question—as currently worded—cannot be answered, you will keep tweaking it until it works. This is part of the thought process for every student. So, in short, please don't think something is wrong if you find yourself revising your question repeatedly. It's actually a sign that you're doing things correctly!

The Seven Attributes of a Usable Research Question

Not all research questions are created equal. As you write your research question, there are some guidelines to keep in mind that will help you stay on track. With every new version of the question you consider, evaluate it based on the following criteria.

1. A research question should invite analysis and interpretation.

Typically (but by no means always), "why" and "how" questions will lead you in the right direction as you think about your topic. When historians ask "why" or "how," they are not asking for a chronology of events, per se, but are engaging in interpretation and debate. On the other hand, a question that asks "what happened" or "what is" will usually call for a list of events. Remember that the purpose of a college-level research paper is not to report on the past, but instead to offer an interpretation of the past that is based on primary source evidence. Similarly, a useful research question should not invite a simple yes or no answer, as it would provide no room to offer an explanation for your idea—and no acknowledgment of the complexity of the past and the role of multiple causality (see pp. 36–38).

The centrality of interpretation as a goal in college-level historical research highlights one way in which the metaphor of the jigsaw puzzle doesn't entirely work as a way of characterizing the research process, or at least needs to be modified. In a typical jigsaw puzzle, there is only one way of putting together the pieces correctly. The pieces of a historical event, by contrast—the many different actors who contributed to it, the many different factors that led to it, the many different forces at work in it—can be put together in many different ways, all of which can potentially yield a compelling final picture. The puzzle of the past, that is, does not and cannot have one single solution. When sifting through and starting to assemble the disparate pieces of the historical topic you are researching, your job is not to look for the one correct way in which they all fit together, but to envision and articulate the way of fitting them together that makes the most sense to you—in other words, to exercise interpretation. The way to get started on this is to ask an interpretive question, one that will get you thinking in terms of causes and contexts rather than facts and chronologies, whys and hows rather than yeses and nos.

2. A research question should use concise, clear language.

The more precise you can be in wording your question, the better off you will be in starting your search for appropriate primary and secondary sources. For instance, students will often first think to ask, "Why did this situation change?" Since the word "change" can be read in multiple ways, it would be better to ask, "Why did this situation worsen?" Or, alternatively, "Why did this situation improve?"

The best way to make sure your question is worded well is to ask a friend or family member to read it and explain, in her own words, what you are planning to investigate. If she gets stuck, you will be able to isolate the word or words that need to be revised in your question in order to improve it.

3. A research question needs to avoid value-laden words.

By "value-laden" words, I am referring to words that cast judgment on something or someone. Frequently used examples are "good," "bad," "successful," or "unsuccessful." As a historian, you want to adopt an even-handed approach to your subject matter. If you approach your topic with preconceived notions of what is "good" or "bad," you will cause others to question your credibility. Typically, it is better to think more carefully about what the words "good" or "bad" really mean in context, and choose more precise language going forward.

4. A research question must avoid speculation.

Some students come up with wonderfully imaginative ideas for research questions, such as "What if John F. Kennedy hadn't been assassinated?" or "What if the Civil War hadn't taken place?" But while it is intriguing to speculate on what could have happened if history had turned out differently than it did, this approach doesn't work in a historical research paper. You have no way of answering these questions because they don't rely on actual facts. Remember that your thesis needs to be defended with primary sources, not imagined stories.

5. A research question should be of reasonable scope.

Are you asking a question that can be answered adequately in the space of your paper's designated number of pages? This is difficult to know at first. What looks like a great question at first may need to be narrowed by the addition of a specific geographical region or a shorter time frame. Or, you might find that there simply isn't enough information available on the topic as you have framed it, requiring you to broaden it to include more sources.

6. A research question can be answered with available sources.

You might have a terrific question that fits criteria 1 through 5. But if you can't access the sources you need to answer it, you won't be able to come up with a thesis statement. It would be like having only half the pieces you need to finish the puzzle, or half the ingredients in a recipe. In order to avoid this problem, make sure at the outset that the primary sources you require can be accessed at your campus library or through the internet, either via commercial databases or digital archives. (Indeed, digitization of primary and secondary sources makes this criterion far easier to satisfy than even fifteen years ago.) Otherwise, you'll be stuck waiting to view your sources, and your entire project will be subject to delay.

7. A research question addresses one issue only.

Some students have trouble narrowing their focus, and submit two research questions at once that are separated by the word "and." Don't make this mistake, because it will only cause you further confusion down the road. This sounds like the simplest rule to follow (and indeed it is), but it is also, in my experience, one of the most frequently violated.

Evaluating Research Questions

You might understand all of the above in theory, but it's another thing to apply these rules in practice. Using the seven criteria listed above, how would you evaluate the following research questions?

- Was the Civil Rights Movement good for African Americans?
- How did President Lincoln help to abolish slavery?
- Why did America get involved in World War II?
- Why was Vietnam an unpopular war, but World War II a popular war?
- Had the United States not restricted immigration in 1924, what might have happened?
- Why did Holocaust rescuers risk their lives to save Jews in Poland?

For each question, determine which rules have been violated. Then, explain how you would recommend the student revise the question to make it a better research tool going forward. Imagine that all questions have been submitted by students who intend to write a ten-page paper.

Below, you'll find my critique of each question and what I suggest the student do to revise it. Note that you may assess these questions differently than I have. What matters is not the specific points of each interpretation, but rather that you are able to see the major stumbling blocks to avoid.

For your convenience, the attributes (or rules) are reprinted below. *Note that you can practice more using other examples of research questions, which can be found on the companion website to this book.*

Attributes of a Research Question

USEFUL RESEARCH QUESTION	PROBLEMATIC RESEARCH QUESTION
1. Invites analysis and interpretation	Asks for a list of events, or yes/no answer
2. Utilizes concise, clear language	Uses vague language
3. Avoids value-laden words	Implies value judgments
4. Avoids speculation	Asks for speculation
5. Is of reasonable scope	Is too narrow or broad
6. Can be answered with sources	Cannot be answered with available sources
7. Consists of one issue only	Consists of more than one issue

- Was the Civil Rights Movement good for African Americans?

This is not a suitable research question because it breaks rules 1, 2, 3, and 5. The initial problem is simply that the question invites a simple yes or no answer (rule 1). It is impossible to know which aspect of the Civil Rights Movement—a complex, multifaceted phenomenon—the student is referring to with this question (rule 1), and they can't possibly describe such a complex historical period in one paper (rule 5). Doing so would surely result in an encyclopedia article, at best. Also, how is the student defining the word "good"? That word needs to be replaced with something far more specific (rules 2 and 3).

Chances are that this student may be interested in evaluating how the Civil Rights Movement helped to advance the freedoms and opportunities of African Americans in the United States and exploring in what ways and to what extent their freedoms and opportunities remain restricted. That type of question might work, but the student must first specify which aspect of the Civil Rights Movement he wishes to study, and then take a careful look at its impact on African Americans. Let's say the student decided to examine the Civil Rights Act of 1964. Their question might work better if it were reworded as follows: "How did the Civil Rights Act of 1964 affect African Americans?" Eventually, the student might decide to determine a time frame to narrow the question further—say, "How did the Civil Rights Act of 1964 affect African Americans in the five years after its implementation?" The choice of the verb "affect" allows the student to craft a thesis that incorporates both the Act's positive contributions and its shortcomings.

You might ask how I determined what aspect of the topic interested the student. Typically, what I usually found is that when students wrote research questions like this one, they had already read or discovered something in the course of their research that intrigued them, but they didn't know how to put it into a question. As a result, they wrote a question in rather generic terms. When asked what motivated them to move in this direction, they provided more detail. Talking things out, in other words, can be a useful strategy to find out what's really motivating you to stick with this topic.

- How did President Lincoln help to abolish slavery?

This research question violates rules 2 and 5. It is a classic example of a research question that is way too vague (rule 2). It does invite interpretation, but would first need to be narrowed to a reasonable scope before it can be useful (rule 5). In advising the student, I would suggest that they first choose a particular measure that illustrated Lincoln's opposition to slavery. With that example in mind, I would encourage the student to work on revising the term "help" so that it provided a clearer indication of Lincoln's political and social contribution to abolitionism. "How did President Lincoln's issuance of the Emancipation Proclamation contribute to the abolition of slavery?" would be a good initial revision of this research question, although it could be sharpened even further.

- Why did America get involved in World War II?

This research question violates rules 1 and 5. Even though it is currently a "why" question, it nevertheless invites a list of reasons that might come from an encyclopedia article on World War II (rule 1). The "grocery list" question is a trap door in writing historical research questions that students need to avoid as it leads to thesis statements that contain lists of reasons. The other problem is that "get involved" is not a phrase that would require much interpretation or critical thinking on the part of the student. Overtly, the US "got involved" in World War II—that is, it became a belligerent in the conflict—for a very clear and specific reason: the Japanese bombing of Pearl Harbor. The answer to this question, as it's currently phrased, is therefore pretty obvious.

This research question is also too broad (rule 5). Rather than examining the perspective of an entire country, the student should look at individual leaders or important stakeholders at the time, and perhaps at the debate surrounding the country's entry into World War II. There was a large segment of American society, for example, that did not support US involvement in the war. Adopting the slogan "America First," they preferred the isolationist approach to the global community that characterized American policy in the 1920s and 1930s.[1]

Alternatively, the student might want to examine the precise moment when the American government made the decision to join the war—immediately after Pearl Harbor in December 1941—and explore the ways in which Americans responded to that decision. Was there any debate in the press? Were President Roosevelt's advisers united in their decision to enter the war, or were there prominent skeptics? Can we access veterans' testimonies regarding their decision to enlist? Was there debate surrounding that decision? As you can see, the student needs to choose a particular moment

1 In 2025, the Trump Administration applied the label "America First" to many aspects of its political agenda. Like any other, the phrase has to be properly situated in its historical context in order to understand its intended meaning and social and political implications. See, for instance, "President Trump's America First Priorities," The White House, January 20, 2025, https://www.whitehouse.gov/briefings-statements/.

in time, or the actions of a particular historical figure (or figures), rather than pursue the vague idea of "involvement" in war in a general sense.

- Why was Vietnam an unpopular war, but World War II a popular war?

This research question violates rules 3 and 5. The first issue that stands out is the word "popular," which is a type of value judgment (rule 3): it leads us to ask what it means for a war to be popular in the first place. Does the student mean that the war won public approval at the time? If so, then with whom, specifically, was it popular? Are we talking about the American perspective? If so, with soldiers or civilians? The first thing this student needs to do is provide some historical context for understanding what we mean by "popularity," and perhaps use another adjective that speaks more specifically to the student's intended meaning. Depending on their perspective, different communities or historical actors can view participation in war as justifiable, worthwhile, noble, or reckless.

The student also has an obligation to narrow the scope of this question (rule 5). "Vietnam" could refer to virtually any, or even all, aspects of the Vietnam War, from the entry of military advisers under President Kennedy to US combat troops' final withdrawal in 1973—a long stretch of time in which Americans' views of the conflict shifted in significant ways. Similarly, World War II of course encompassed—from America's perspective—two different military theaters and four years of fighting. The student must decide which elements of each war are of primary interest.

If the student were more curious about historians' perspectives on each war, it might be possible to give the question a slightly broader focus. In this case, the student should go back to their secondary sources and figure out what historians have actually said and are saying about each conflict, then replace the word "popular" with something that more accurately represents the scholars' perspectives.

- Had the United States not restricted immigration in 1924, what might have happened?

This question clearly violates rule 4: it engages in speculation about what would have happened if history had not taken place as it did. Simply put, this is not a viable option in historical research papers because the question is entirely imaginative.

Students frequently get very disappointed when they learn that this type of counter-factual inquiry won't work as a viable research question. It's important to point out that plenty of great novels, TV shows, and other works of fiction take a scenario like this and run with it quite successfully. The issue is that these are works of *fiction*. This type of question is not something that can form the foundation of a historical research paper, which is based on facts and the historian's interpretation of those facts.

- Why did Holocaust rescuers risk their lives to save Jews in Poland?

This question potentially violates rules 5 and 6. The student first needs to understand that people who rescued Jews during the Holocaust were a highly diverse group who made the decision to do so for a variety of reasons. Depending on the location and time period, rescuers may have faced dramatically different circumstances, may have acted alone or with larger groups, and so forth. Grouping everyone together in this way makes it sound as if one narrative can define all rescuers, which it certainly cannot (rule 5).

This question also suggests that the researcher needs sources that will enable her to answer the question posed (rule 6). Most likely, the student will need primary sources, including interviews or memoirs, which provide insight into the rescuers' reasons or motivations for deciding to save Jews. Reliable documentation of the motivations or intentions of individual people in the past is frequently difficult to come by—particularly so when it comes to so fraught and perilous a decision as protecting Jews during the Holocaust. In lieu of a sufficient number of reliable primary sources, we know what happened but cannot necessarily answer the question of why.

This is an excellent example of a question requiring a student to check primary sources first, in order to make sure that the question can be answered with the sources available. Most likely, the student's research will be driven by the body of primary sources they can access in the time frame they have to do research. An additional factor that comes into play here is the language in which the sources are written. Researching topics in Holocaust history, for instance, often requires knowledge of German or Polish if the primary sources haven't been translated into English.

See Online Companion Exercise for Chapter 5
sites.broadviewpress.com/puzzle/chapter-5

Strategies for Writing and Revising Your Research Question

Now you are probably thinking, "Great! With all of these rules, how will I manage to write my own research question in a way that actually works?" This response is completely understandable. Students often intellectually grasp the problems associated with research questions presented to them as bad examples, but have trouble applying the same type of critique to their own work. A number of strategies might help get you started in making this transition.

Be prepared to revise your question. This strategy bears repeating. Recognize from the start that this will not be a one-step process. You will need to rewrite, and then refine, your research question a number of times before you arrive at something that will work for your project. Just anticipate that going into this process, so that you don't feel like you're failing if it's harder than you expected.

Start with your sources and see what they suggest. Though we will talk about evaluating sources in the next chapter, recognize that the research process is not linear. We often have to move back and forth between our primary and secondary sources and our research question in order to see what strategy for framing the project makes the most sense. For the questions about America getting involved in World War II and Holocaust rescuers risking their lives to save Jews in Poland, for instance, I suggested that students consult available sources first in order to help rewrite the question. If your current research question simply isn't practical given what you've found to work with so far, you'd be wise to shift gears.

This point merits additional emphasis. Though this book lays out research "steps" in a seemingly straightforward, linear fashion, by all means recognize that you may need to go back and forth when actually moving through your project. (See the bidirectional arrows on the chart on page 20).

Create a general paper outline based on your question. One of the best ways to see if your question can work is to simply try to answer it! On one page, sketch out a series of subheadings that would define the main sections of your paper if the current research question were employed, and ask yourself where the gaps are. Using what you currently know about your topic, you should be able to figure out where the problems lie.

With a friend as a sounding board, test your question against each of the rules, individually. Since we often find it much easier to evaluate work that is not our own, this is a great time to ask a classmate or family member to listen as you explain what you are hoping to learn in the course of your research. Systematically, review each rule and indicate how your question invites interpretation, is of appropriate scope, and so on. Ask your friend to provide feedback on whatever is unclear, to ask questions, etc. If you get stuck somewhere along the way, that's a clue that you might need to revise your research question slightly for it to work.

Let it sit. This is a good example of how it can help tremendously to not be pressured by an imminent deadline. If you find yourself unable to view your research question with a critical eye, concentrate on something else for twenty-four to forty-eight hours and revisit it when you can give it a fresh look. You'll be impressed by how much it helps to reevaluate something after taking a break from it. However, this will prove absolutely impossible if you've waited until the last minute because you won't have forty-eight hours to work with.

CHAPTER 6

Evaluating Historical Sources

As you become more certain of the direction your research is taking, you'll need to start looking for sources. Historians rely on two types of sources when they conduct research, mentioned briefly earlier in this book: *primary* and *secondary*. You may be familiar with these categories already, but in this chapter we'll review them in some depth. We'll also discuss specific types of questions that you need to think about when working with historical sources so that you can be sure you're using them appropriately for research purposes.

Distinguishing between Primary and Secondary Sources

Depending on the particular course you are taking and the particular branch of history you are studying, you will probably be expected to consult a variety of primary and secondary sources during your research. *Primary sources* come directly from the era you are researching. They are firsthand accounts from which you can access voices from the period under investigation. *Secondary sources*, on the other hand, are accounts written about the past, typically by historians or scholars in a related discipline (anthropologists, sociologists, or ethnographers, for instance). If you find journal articles or books written within the last ten to fifteen years, they are most likely secondary. Secondary sources are one step removed from the historical period in question.

A subset of secondary sources is referred to as *tertiary*. Examples of tertiary sources include encyclopedias, almanacs, and chronologies. Tertiary sources are most helpful when you are first starting out in your research and need general, background information on a broad topic or range of topics. However, college instructors typically do not count tertiary sources in the minimum number of sources required for a paper. Instead, these sources serve primarily as tools to help you get up to speed on your topic.

See Online Companion Exercise 6A
sites.broadviewpress.com/puzzle/chapter-6

Primary Sources

EXAMPLES OF PRIMARY SOURCES: THE STUFF OF HISTORY

When I taught about primary sources, I found it helpful to ask students to think about what was in their parents' attic or basement. If you have a "saver" in your family (and many people fit the bill!), you probably have stuff that has been around for a long time and is gathering dust. If you think about the different kinds of things you might find if you opened up a box in the attic or basement, you'll have a good idea of what primary sources are: personal letters; a diary; newspaper clippings; family photographs; wall hangings; a driver's license from a great-grandparent; a military dog tag; a magazine advertisement for a local business; sheet music for a song composed by the family musician; an old grocery store list; a classified ad; a tool box from the 1930s; a favorite childhood toy that's now considered a collectible; a novel published in 1955. The list is endless.

Now imagine that you visit a local non-profit organization, be it a church or synagogue, or a charitable organization that raises money for a particular cause. If you went to the basement of that building, you might find old furniture from a boardroom that has since been renovated; file cabinets containing meeting minutes from the time of the organization's founding; the zoning application for a church to use a property for religious purposes; plaques with pictures of past presidents; brochures distributed at the organization's tenth anniversary party; or copies of letters to supporters asking for donations. Maybe you'll find interoffice correspondence, or boxes of old stationery from the organization when it was housed at a different location.

Lastly, picture your visit to a government office building. You might find local census records; birth certificates; Social Security applications; zoning records or real estate development plans for urban neighborhoods, and so on. You might uncover audio recordings of meetings held long ago, before video recordings were available.

Most (though not all) of what you'll uncover in these dark, dusty corners are primary sources and might be of great value to historians. As you can see from the above list of items, primary sources can be textual, visual (such as pictures or videos), or even objects. Professional historians often choose to focus most of their attention on one particular type of source, depending on their area of interest, but finding and studying a great variety of primary sources can be a very evocative way of bringing to life the distinct texture of a particular past era.

WHERE OTHER PRIMARY SOURCES LIVE

Thankfully, for those of us who don't love hanging around in musty basements or attics, individuals or institutions sometimes decide to donate their possessions to historical archives. Archives are institutions which house primary sources so that scholars and other interested parties can access them easily in a safe and secure environment. Archivists are professionals trained to sort through and organize collections of sources and create finding aids, print or digital guides to the items in each collection.

Many libraries, whether public or affiliated with colleges and universities, contain archival divisions. Your university library likely contains some archival collections that document the early years of the institution. You might find old course syllabi, yearbooks, and perhaps curricular guides of courses and times for a particular semester. You might also find copies of the university newspaper, which provides insight into what was happening on campus. You may also be familiar with your town, state, or province's archives, or perhaps, most famously, the National Archives in Washington, DC, which contains the founding documents of the United States.

When I was a college student in the early 1990s, most archival sources were completely inaccessible to students, unless you were lucky enough to live close to the institution you wanted to visit. The only way we could read newspaper articles from an earlier era was to use a microfilm machine, scanning for hours and spending a small fortune to print copies at twenty-five to fifty cents per page! Some of those pages were, invariably, impossible to read when printed, making the research process expensive and potentially quite frustrating! And if you were lucky enough to have access to a physical copy of a newspaper, you'd keep your fingers crossed, hoping the page didn't crumble to pieces when you handled it.

Today, many archives worldwide have digitized at least some of their primary sources and made them available for public consumption on the internet. Thanks to these digital archives, one can access in minutes newspapers and magazines dating back to the nineteenth century or earlier, all without leaving your home! (Can you tell I'm very excited about this? Or that I'm really old? Your choice.) Such technological innovations have made historical research much easier for students, who now can access a broad range of sources that were completely inaccessible just fifteen or twenty years ago. In the next chapter we'll discuss some techniques for finding primary sources online.

You'll still probably find many of your primary sources in books in your university library. Shorter sources on a particular topic are often published together in anthologies or "readers." Typically, each selection in an anthology is considered a separate source and must be cited separately in your paper's bibliography. (Just in case, check with your instructor to see if you could abbreviate the entries for primary sources from one volume.) Primary source readers often contain very helpful introductions that provide historical background and context. If you are studying the history of a non-English-speaking country or region, or an older historical period (e.g., the Middle Ages), primary source readers—in particular, collections of translated primary sources—will be especially useful (and perhaps crucial if you don't know the language(s) in which the sources were originally written).

QUESTIONS TO ASK OF SOURCES: THE HISTORIAN'S BURDEN

Now that we have surveyed the primary sources you can choose from, let's discuss the burden on the historian to analyze them. Why do you have to read your sources carefully and represent them fairly? The image below should help explain the answer.

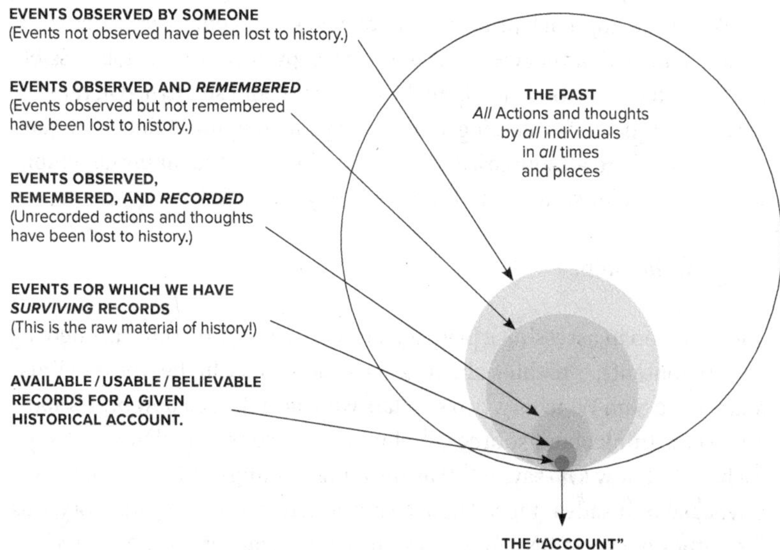

From *The Methods and Skills of History* by Conal Furay.
Reprinted by permission of Wiley Publishing; all rights reserved.

If we think of the entire sphere as reflecting every action or event that has ever happened ("the past"), we move down each level to arrive at the small fraction of historical events that not only took place, but were also observed, remembered, and recorded. An even smaller subset includes sources for which credible records *actually exist and are available.* Since we have so little to work with when explaining the past, we must be very careful to use our sources wisely. We can only make assertions about the past when adequate sources exist to support those assertions. We need to approach our primary sources in particular with the utmost care, and not give any individual source more weight that it deserves. For me, at least, this diagram serves as the most explicit way of demonstrating the problems of making broad generalizations in history papers without appropriate evidence to support them.

In order to exercise appropriate caution in studying history, professional historians get in the habit of *asking questions of sources.* By asking questions, we're able to keep track of what a source can and cannot tell us—what it contributes to our understanding of the past, and what its shortcomings may be. A general rule of thumb that I like to teach my students is that *no source is perfect.* Every historical source contributes something to the bigger picture, in other words, but also has significant limitations.

When you approach primary sources, you should put your detective hat on and read with a very critical eye. Make a copy of your source, if possible, so that you can write on it, highlight key words, and so forth. (Or, take the parallel approach if evaluating a source on your computer.) Not every question will apply to all sources, and there may be more that apply depending on the particular source, but these will get you started.

1. Authorship.

The first step in assessing a primary source, before you even start delving into its contents, is to think about who its author was. In the words of Daisy Martin and Sam Wineburg, two scholars who have studied how professional historians think about sources, "Before we can consider what a text says, we have to know *who* says it."[1] Was the author young or old? Economically privileged or disadvantaged? If race or ethnicity matters to your story, was the author white, African American, Hispanic, Asian, or Indigenous? What religion were they? From what country and region did they come? What was their political viewpoint? What was their occupation? Were they an activist or a reactionary? Try to find out as much as possible about the authors or

1 Daisy Martin and Sam Wineburg, "Seeing Thinking on the Web," *The History Teacher* 41, no. 3 (May 2008): 313, www.jstor.org/stable/30036914.

creators of your sources, even if it means looking up their name in online encyclopedias or in secondary sources that might mention them. If you have an anonymous source, try to get any clues you can from the source itself or its context (i.e., where and when it was created, the circumstances of its publication, etc.) as to its author's identity and background. If there are multiple authors involved, see what you can learn about as many of them as possible. If you are looking at a film as a primary source, or a film clip, try to get to know something about the director. If you are looking at a photograph, find out more about the photographer, their subject interests, and where their photographs were published.

2. Message.

Try to figure out what the source is telling you. This is the time to circle important words and to look them up if you don't know what they mean. Be prepared to read a primary source multiple times if it is extremely important to your research, as often as needed in order to internalize the meaning of a document. If the author's message is complicated, break it down by making notes in the margin of the document (or in a separate file on your computer), tracking the author's progression from point to point. If you are having difficulty understanding the meaning of a document, by all means email your professor with your question. Set up a time to meet if necessary and review the document with them in person.

Just as important for understanding the author's message is the need to suspend your own judgments or criticism regarding it. This can be very hard to do, especially if you, as a twenty-first-century reader, disagree strongly with the perspective adopted in the source. Record your own opinions in a different color pen (or font, if you're typing) so that you can distinguish between your own views and those represented in the account.

3. Audience.

By audience, I mean the intended readers or viewers. For instance, if you are examining a recently declassified document from the US State Department, it might have been intended for a very small audience of politicians and bureaucrats at a very specific time. A private letter found in a box in your parents' attic most likely had only one intended reader. But the transcript of a politician's speech, for example, is something that would have been accessible to many, and was likely a public document.

If you are reading a newspaper editorial, try to determine the likely perspective of the newspaper's readership based on geography, political leanings, social viewpoints, and so forth. If you are examining an advertisement in a magazine, think about who would have subscribed to that periodical and who might have been most likely to buy the product. If you're watching a 1960s TV ad for a political candidate, look for clues regarding who the ad was targeting.

Remember that before the digital age, publishers, producers, and directors reached target audiences based on who would buy their magazine or tune in to their television show. There was no such thing as binge-watching a Netflix series on a computer; there were no blog posts or social media sites with links to your favorite articles. A lot of planning and strategizing went into the decision of how to reach target audiences, because there was only one opportunity to do so.

4. Context.

No primary source was produced in a vacuum. It's your responsibility to try to find out as much as possible about your source. If you don't have a date for the source, find clues within it so that you can make your best guess. If you're looking at a protest song that was sung at rallies during the Civil Rights Movement, find out what happened in the city or town where your source was created just before that song was written, and what was going on socio-politically at the time.

5. Motivation.

Why was this source created? What event or cause inspired its production or creation? When we think about motivation, we get a sense of the author's or creator's explicit purpose or intent. Again, let's think about photographs in this context. Some photojournalists took pictures with the goal of drawing national attention to a particular problem, such as racial inequality in America or the horrors of the Vietnam War. Other photographs or films, however, were created with the aim of legitimizing particular policies or regimes—think, for example, of Leni Riefenstahl's infamous propaganda films glorifying Hitler and the Nazi regime in Germany.

Motivation is particularly interesting in the context of autobiographies or memoirs. The decision to publish one's life story—or a carefully constructed version of one's life story—is not a decision that most of us will ever make. Those who do so clearly have a sense that what they have to share is important enough to make public. The larger question is why. Is this an issue of passing on a particular legacy to one's descendants? However defined, how might the author's motivation for writing affect the way the source was written?

6. Bias.

Motivation is inextricably tied to the author's or creator's bias—the perspective represented by the source. Virtually every source has a bias of some sort; the only exception that comes to mind would be a report of data, such as sports scores ("Orioles 4, Yankees 2"—though fans of the losing team may disagree with me). Because our sources are inherently biased, we need to try to access as many different perspectives on the same event as possible. That's the only way to minimize the extent to which our own interpretation of sources is biased in favor of one perspective over another.

A picture is biased depending on the wishes or agenda of the photographer. The example I always think of is when a politician or other public figure is photographed from the perspective of a person looking up at them in the audience, as if to show that they are larger than life. Clearly the camera has just as much bias as a writer; it's just expressed differently.

One approach to assessing a source that can help clarify its biases—even or especially its unconscious biases—is what Daisy Martin and Sam Wineburg call "reading the silences." In order to read the silences of a source, ask yourself questions such as "What is the speaker *not* mentioning? Whose voices are we *not* hearing in a particular document or historical account? Which perspectives are missing?" Martin and Wineburg give the example of one historian to whom they showed a senatorial campaign speech from 1898 (an era the historian was not a specialist in) that characterized America's westward expansion as "carr[ying] the flag across the blazing deserts and through the ranks of hostile mountains." The historian noted that, according to the speech, "'It was the mountains that were hostile,' not the actual people living there. 'It was the continent that was overrun,' not the civilizations that occupied it."[2] The speech, in other words, was *silent* about the presence of the Indigenous peoples who dwelt on the land being colonized. By detecting and interrogating this silence, the historian was able to uncover a significant bias in the speech's perspective on American westward expansion.

2 Martin and Wineburg, "Seeing Thinking on the Web," 310–11.

You can read the silences of visual sources, too. A photograph, for example, is by definition a snapshot in time, and photographs only include some things by excluding others. It is essential to know what the photographer might have left out. Would the people or things omitted from the photograph have dramatically changed its nature if they had been included?

7. Response.

What kind of reception did the source receive when it was produced? The word "response" is most frequently associated with the publication of a novel or the release of a film—was it praised, denigrated, or criticized? But we can also think of a "response" to a letter. How might this source have been read by the intended audience, and what might members of that audience have thought about it or done in response to it?

The tricky aspect of this category is that we don't often know for sure what the response actually was, and instead must rely on clues. Nevertheless, by considering the question of response in connection with all of the other issues, it may be possible to make an informed guess.

8. Absence.

What might you have expected to read in your source that you *didn't* actually find? Is there a topic you assumed would be addressed but wasn't? What figures would you have expected to have shown up in your visual source but were absent? Addressing issues of absence is a little different from the other categories, because ultimately it involves thinking about yourself, as a historian, and the set of assumptions that you bring to the table, and how they differ from what you uncover in a primary document. Your notes on this section will probably be most relevant to you when you've thought about what other sources you'll need to complement this one.

Absence is closely related to the silences alluded to in our discussion of bias above, but relates more to the perspective we bring to the table as contemporary readers.

9. Surprise.

Similar to absence in some ways, the "surprise" category requires you to think about what caught your eye when examining a primary source for the first time. What jumped out at you about this source? What defied your expectations or struck you as unusual? Why do you find this aspect of the source surprising? What questions does this aspect of the source raise about your research focus? Does it help to answer, or begin to answer, your research question?

As implied here, your notes on what surprises you about a source will likely evolve over time as you learn more about your topic as your thesis develops. You might even find that what struck you as unusual on a first reading makes a good deal more sense as you gain greater familiarity with your subject matter. Don't be afraid to revisit your comments on a source later in the research process to see how your ideas have changed over time.

10. Credibility.

Is this source trustworthy? Is there anything that makes you doubt its authenticity? Sometimes such doubts arise if no author has been provided, or if you are not quite sure where or how a source originated. If you have this concern, you should be careful to find at least one other source (preferably more than one) that corroborates or confirms what you think you learned in this source. You can't draw conclusions from a source whose credibility you doubt.

Below are a sample primary source and some abbreviated notes taken in response to the ten questions listed above. For your reference, these questions are summarized in the chart below.

Ten Questions to Ask of Primary Sources

CRITERION	QUESTION TO ASK
1. Authorship	Who wrote/created this source?
2. Message	What is the most basic message to take from this source, and how is it presented?
3. Audience	Who was the source written for?
4. Context	In what context was the source written (social, geographical, political, etc.)?
5. Motivation	Why was this source created?
6. Bias	In what way is this source inherently biased?
7. Response	What kind of response did this source receive from those who encountered it at the time?
8. Absence	What is left out of this source that I expected to see?
9. Surprise	What surprised me about this source when I read/examined it?
10. Credibility	Is this source credible? Is there any chance this source may not be credible?

A Sample Primary Source Analysis

Context: The 19th Amendment was passed in 1920 and granted women in the United States the right to vote. The debate on the issue leading up to that point was heated and divisive, as suggested by the document below. It is a portion of a pamphlet distributed in the 1910s by the National Association Opposed to Woman Suffrage.

Housewives! [page 2]

You do not need a ballot to clean out your sink spout. A handful of potash and some boiling water is quicker and cheaper.

If new tinware be rubbed all over with fresh lard, then thoroughly heated before using, it will never rust.

Use oatmeal on a damp cloth to clean white paint.

Control of the temper makes a happier home than control of elections.

When boiling fish or fowls, add juice of half a lemon to the water to prevent discoloration.

Celery can be freshened by being left over night in a solution of salt and water.

Good cooking lessens alcoholic craving quicker than a vote.

Why vote for pure food laws, when your husband does that, while you can purify your ice-box with saleratum water?

Common sense and common salt applications stop hemorrhage quicker than ballots....

Sulpho naphthol and elbow grease drive out bugs quicker than hot political air....

Clean houses and good homes, which cannot be provided by legislation, keep children healthier and happier than any number of uplift laws.

Butter on a fresh burn take out the sting. But what removes the sting of political defeat?

Vote NO on Woman Suffrage [page 4]

BECAUSE 90% of the women either do not want it, or *do not care.*

BECAUSE it means *competition* of women with men instead of *co-operation.*

BECAUSE 80% of the women eligible to vote are married and can only double or annul their husband's votes.

BECAUSE it can be of no benefit commensurate with the additional expense involved....

BECAUSE it is unwise to risk the good we already have for the evil which may occur.

Source: "Pamphlet by the National Association Opposed to Woman Suffrage," Jewish Women's Archive, accessed March 16, 2025, http://jwa.org/media/pamphlet-distributed-by-national-association-opposed-to-woman-suffrage.

Notes on Anti-Suffrage Document

1. **Authorship**—*What else did this group put out? Who were the leaders?*
2. **Message**—*Domestic role for women, which did not include political rights.*
3. **Audience**—*Housewives, mothers (white? Middle/upper class?)—Would minorities have been included here?*
4. **Context**—*Most people wanted an amendment at this point, so they were outliers. How many other organizations had this perspective? Did those groups make their points of views known to the public?*
5. **Motivation**—*To make women think voting was not appropriate for them: to make women think domestic work was the most important job.*
6. **Bias**—*They'd have no reason to give credence to women suffragists.*
7. **Response**—*Not sure based on this document. Check* NY Times *and* Washington Post *issues from the 1910s for any mention of this organization.*
8. **Absence**—*Look at the rest of the pamphlet for more references to men's roles, and what they believe.*
9. **Surprise**—*Where do the percentages come from? Proof that this was true? What expense are they talking about? Why do they see women only in relation to their husbands instead of as individuals, if both could potentially have the vote?*
10. **Credibility**—*Not in question.*

See Online Companion Exercise 6B
sites.broadviewpress.com/puzzle/chapter-6

Secondary Sources

THE IMPORTANCE OF CURRENCY

No, I don't mean money. By currency, I'm saying that secondary sources are best if the interpretation they offer is current—that is, if it is still accepted, or considered legitimate, by scholars. Any source you choose should have been written in the past few decades, particularly if you're dealing with a recent historical event. Historical writing and interpretation (historiography) change and evolve over time (see the explanation of historiography in Chapter 1, pp. 5–6). For example, someone writing about US involvement in the Vietnam War in 2024 has a very different understanding than someone writing in 1994—to say nothing of someone who wrote in 1964!

Don't make the mistake of ignoring a secondary source's publication date. It is imperative that you be certain that your secondary source be far enough removed from the historical period you're studying to be considered reliable, but is also recent enough that the interpretations it offers haven't been superseded or deemed outdated.

THE RANGE OF OPTIONS

Let's begin by previewing the types of secondary sources that students most frequently use in writing a college research paper.

Books. Most of your sources for a historical research paper will likely be books that you check out of your campus library and/or e-books. For the most part, you will want to stick with books that were published by university presses (University Press of New England, Yale University Press, and so forth), as these are written by scholars and peer-reviewed—that is, vetted by other qualified scholars for the accuracy of their facts and the cogency and currency of their interpretations. For a historical paper, you should try to find books written by professional historians or by experts in a related field of study such as anthropology, sociology, or political science. Journalists also frequently write on historical topics, and many journalist-authored history books are authoritatively researched and highly regarded. That said, the perspectives and agendas of journalists often differ significantly from those of academic historians.

You will especially want to find at least a few *monographs* on your research topic. Historians use the word "monograph" to refer to full-length books on one topic (often by a single author) that are published by university presses, are based on archival primary sources, take into account relevant secondary sources written on the topic, and are meant to contribute *new* knowledge. Monographs are going to be among your most useful and reputable secondary sources. (By contrast, other kinds of books, especially textbooks, are meant to synthesize and repackage existing historical knowledge. Monographs should also be distinguished from books published by trade presses—that is, publishers not affiliated with universities and whose books are meant for the general public rather than for scholars. Unlike monographs, some trade publications, even if they are written by academic historians, may not have been peer-reviewed.)

If a book you've found looks like it is on-topic and has a reputable publisher and author, check if it has footnotes or endnotes and a bibliography (or "Works Cited") of sources consulted. Most publishers of historical books require citations to be included, and their inclusion is a sign that the book is appropriate for your paper. The presence of citations, in other words, demonstrates that the author had to adhere to conventions of history writing. Were you to try to look up something that is mentioned in the book, you could use the citation to identify where the author found their information. It's also very helpful to consult a book's index and look up key terms in order to determine to what extent they are addressed in the book, which in turn will determine how useful the book will be for your research.

RED FLAG ALERT: Stay away from books intended for adolescent or juvenile audiences. I had dozens of students include books in their bibliographies that were actually written for children. While these books are often on the shelves of your public or university library, they really have no place in a college-level paper. Written with very young readers in mind, they necessarily minimize issues of historical complexity and nuance. When students include these types of sources in their bibliographies despite being told that they are inappropriate, they are revealing that they have not yet retrieved the books from the library. Or, alternatively, they have done so and either are trying to pad their bibliography, or have not carefully evaluated the sources they're reading for their appropriateness.

Sources within edited collections. You may also consult essays that are collected in one volume because they all deal with the same historical topic or theme. Typically, each essay has been written by a different author. Usually, you'll find that essay collections also contain an introduction written by the collection's editor (or editors) that discusses the essays' shared themes. Each essay in the volume would be its own secondary source. Essay collections published by university presses are also peer-reviewed and reputable.

Journal articles. In your library's commercial databases, you'll have access to academic journal articles that—like monographs and edited essay collections—have been subject to peer review. This means that in order to be published in that journal, an author must first submit her article to a team of scholars so it can be reviewed and critiqued.

Online articles. You might also find secondary sources from websites, but make sure you choose these very wisely. Verify that they are by authors with academic training in history or a related discipline. It helps to find articles that are listed on websites associated with universities or museums. You will find more guidelines on evaluating websites in Chapter 7.

Videos. Documentaries that provide factual overviews are excellent secondary sources, provided they have been made and distributed by legitimate organizations. Prior to using a YouTube video, track down the director or sponsoring organization to make sure the video has been produced by reputable professionals, rather than by amateurs without expertise in the subject area.

DISTINGUISHING SCHOLARLY SECONDARY SOURCES FROM POPULAR SOURCES

When you are looking for secondary sources online, be especially careful to make sure that you are able to tell the difference between sources appropriate for an academic paper and sources meant for a popular audience. Scholarly articles are intended for use when doing research for an academic paper, while most popular sources really aren't. Here are some distinguishing characteristics to keep in mind.[3]

Popular sources are much shorter than scholarly sources and may contain advertisements or glossy photographs. Remember that journal articles written by historians are usually about fifteen to twenty pages long. An article of only two or three pages is typically not meant for an academic paper. You simply can't expect the same depth from a brief article in a popular magazine.

Popular articles contain few, if any, citations. Unlike the monographs we discussed earlier in this chapter, you will very seldom find footnotes in popular articles. The problem here is that, without citations, you would not be able to trace the author's consulted sources and thus be unable to verify that the author's assertions are correct, or at least defensible.

Popular sources are usually written by journalists rather than scholars from a particular discipline. Typically, papers written in an academic setting require you to cite authors with academic training in a subject area. While journalists are often knowledgeable, they don't have to be experts in history. Unless noted otherwise, you cannot assume that a journalist writing a shorter piece has the appropriate credentials needed for citation in academic writing.

Popular sources do not contain an abstract, while scholarly sources often do. An abstract is a summary of an article's main points and appears at the very beginning of an academic essay. Abstracts are helpful to researchers who have limited time and need to quickly determine if an article is relevant to their research interests.

---

3 "Popular, Scholarly, Trade: What's the Difference?," posted September 4, 2020, by Albert S. Cook Library, YouTube, 9 min., 20 sec., www.youtube.com/watch?v=gTHfugp8tJE&t=3s.

Popular sources are written in simpler language, while scholarly articles may use jargon familiar to academics in a particular field. While academic jargon might initially deter you from engaging closely with a source that uses it (there are plenty of problems with the overuse of jargon in some academic writing), such language does indicate that its author is a specialist writing for other specialists—and as someone undertaking a historical research project, your job is to become such a specialist yourself! This more complex language of scholarly articles also goes hand-in-hand with the fact that, compared to popular sources intended for general audiences, scholarly articles include more nuance and detail. The good news is that compared with scholarly writing in most disciplines, historical writing is far less jargon-heavy and should be reasonably accessible.

READING SECONDARY SOURCES CRITICALLY

When reading secondary sources, you need to keep in mind a very different set of questions than when you analyze primary sources. Your chief goal should be to identify the historian's central argument, or the interpretation of the topic they are studying, and evaluate its merits. Unlike tertiary sources, which are intended to provide broad overviews, secondary sources written by historians advance a particular argument or interpretation of a topic. They are not merely relaying facts, but rather trying to persuade their readers of a particular way of understanding the past, using relevant primary sources as evidence.

Put another way, a historian's objective in writing an essay or monograph is essentially the same as yours in writing a research paper—but on a much broader scale. Just as you must identify the research question that will frame your investigation and then find relevant sources that will help you formulate a thesis, a historian recognizes or identifies a problem, shortcoming, or unanswered question in existing historical scholarship (historiography) and tries to solve it by using appropriate evidence to advance their argument. When reading secondary sources, you'll need to keep these objectives in mind and look for the ways in which the author achieves them.

Remember these six points as you get started:

1. *You're not reading a novel.* Reading a scholarly article or monograph is far different than reading a mystery or suspense thriller. You won't need to wait until the end to find out what happens. On the contrary, a good work of scholarship should

make clear early on what its argument is and why that argument matters, and then develop and hone that argument in the rest of the work.

2. *You don't need to read the whole book, necessarily.* In order to gather evidence that would enable you to write a short research paper, you'll be reading selectively.
3. *Introductions and conclusions are your friends.* Allow me to formally introduce you to two extraordinarily useful resources: a book's (or article's) introduction and conclusion. Historians put a tremendous amount of important information in them, so please read and re-read them.
4. *Bibliographies and footnotes matter.* You will need to become increasingly aware of these resources, as they tell you precisely what sources the author consulted throughout their research. Should you wish to track down any of the same materials for your own project, you'll want to follow their lead.
5. *Write down page numbers.* Whether you are taking notes on a computer or by hand, please get in the habit of writing down the page numbers whenever you quote, summarize, or paraphrase from a source. You'll thank yourself later when you can actually go back to what you've written and save yourself hours of frustration in looking through your sources (trust me, I've been there many times—it's not fun, especially in the wee hours of the morning).
6. *Distinguish your own views from those of the author.* If you wish to comment on, or disagree with, a point the author makes, consider putting your own views in a different color or font than the rest of your notes. That way you'll be able to distinguish your views from those of the author.

GUIDELINES FOR READING A HISTORICAL MONOGRAPH

Begin by skimming the table of contents, introduction, and conclusion. If you determine that the book you are previewing is something you'd like to use (even just one chapter or section of it), you'll need to figure out the general framework the author is bringing to bear on your topic. A quick overview of the introduction, table of contents, and conclusion will give you a sense of how useful a book will be to your research.

Next, focus on the introduction in more depth. Get a sense of the basic historical context. Ask yourself what the writer is concerned about. Like a journalist, figure out the "who, what, when, where, why, and how" for this book. Keep in mind that you don't need to take down every detail. Write down the terms you might need to look up and the dates of important events. These might also be useful when you search for other primary and secondary sources.

Identify the research problem. For a book-length study, the research problem is the central reason that the author wrote a book. It's analogous to the research question you are thinking about for your paper. In the case of a book, it's the fundamental dilemma that the historian is trying to resolve in the course of his or her writing. The historian's job is to spell that out in the introduction or the book's introductory chapter.

The research problem might take various forms. Here are some common examples:

- *New primary sources are available on a topic.* While few topics haven't been investigated in some way or another, it isn't at all uncommon for a historian to be the first to explore a set of primary sources. Scores of new documents await historical study, inviting the potential for new scholarship. If the book you're examining was written for this reason, the historian will probably spend a bit of time in the introduction describing the collection of sources used to complete the project and why they matter.
- *A gap exists in the historiography.* Sometimes, authors will write books because they feel that current scholarship on a topic does not adequately address a particular aspect of that topic. The primary sources might be readily available, but the existing scholarship in some way skims over them, sidesteps them, or ignores them. The historian undertakes their study in order to close this gap, or at least start the process of doing so.
- *The historiography is out of date.* As time passes, our perspective on historical events changes and evolves, yielding new and—sometimes—more sophisticated understandings and interpretations of those events. Look for discussion like this in your author's introduction if their study aims to provide a new direction for the historiography on their chosen topic.
- *The historian disagrees with arguments currently prevalent in scholarly sources.* Another likely motivating force for a monograph is simply the historian's sense that current interpretations of their subject matter are faulty in some way. They may want to dispute the arguments of another historian or group of historians. If this

is the case, make note of the rival historian(s): you'll likely want to consult their work (or works) in order to understand both sides of this debate.

Identify the thesis. Your next task should be to figure out the author's general argument in the book. Some key words that will help you find the argument might include "prove," "demonstrate," "illustrate," or, simply, "argue." Monographs may have theses that are explained in either one sentence or a short paragraph.

Determine the types of evidence used. Try to figure out what primary sources, or source collections, your author is relying upon to make their argument. When noting the author's thesis, ask yourself if the evidence used makes sense for proving that thesis.

Preview the book structure, if possible. Sometimes, a historian will indicate what to expect in the chapters to come. If this is the case, you should make note of the chapters most relevant to your research topic.

Read relevant chapters only, noting the author's main points. These should, of course, relate to the book's overall thesis.

Read the conclusion. Does the author's thesis, as stated in the introduction, match what is argued in the conclusion? If not, this may not be a clearly written book, or there may be flaws in the overall argument.

See Online Companion Exercise 6C
sites.broadviewpress.com/puzzle/chapter-6

HOW TO READ A JOURNAL ARTICLE OR ACADEMIC ESSAY

A very similar process applies to taking notes on a journal article or an academic essay in an edited collection. Ideally, however, you should only look at journal articles when you have a pretty clear notion of your research question. Why? Journal articles deal with very specific aspects of historical subjects, offering in-depth analyses as opposed to the broader coverage of larger subjects undertaken in monographs. They're intended for a relatively narrow audience who already have at least some background on a topic. If you look at a journal article before you know much about your topic, you might get confused and frustrated.

Start with the abstract, if applicable. An abstract is a summary of an author's main scholarly contribution—the argument they are making and their reasons for making it—that appears at the beginning of the article. The abstract might also include the evidence the historian uses to make their point. Not all historical journals require abstracts, however, so you won't always be able to use this resource.

Devote most of your attention to the article's introduction. In the first two pages or so of a journal article, the historian is obligated to provide a good deal of relevant information. Focus on four main areas that should be spelled out in the introduction:

1. *Historical context.* What is the author discussing? (See pp. 34–38.) Remember that given the shorter length of the article, you should be able to isolate the relevant context pretty quickly.
2. *Research problem.* What motivated the author to write the article? Why is it important? Consult the examples above (pp. 73–74) for some idea of what to look for. In journal articles, though, historians may employ another approach to get a lot of information across quickly. I call this the conventional wisdom approach. They begin with what most scholars believe about a certain topic—a common interpretation, for example—before stating that there's something inherently wrong with that approach, which they proceed to correct in the course of the article.
3. *Thesis.* The author's main argument will most likely appear at the end of the introduction, just before the body of the article begins. In most cases it should appear in one sentence, or at most two or three.
4. *Evidence.* What types of sources does the author use to prove their point? Historians may vary a great deal on how much detail they provide on evidence in their introduction, so be prepared to look further for sources used if necessary.

Read the conclusion to make sure it is consistent with the argument stated in the introduction (see pp. 72–74).

Note that it will take a good bit of practice to become adept at reading journal articles and identifying the relevant information. Students often find this quite challenging at first. If you find it hard to read journal articles, you are in very good company. This is another good time to ask your instructor for help if needed. Below you'll find a sample journal article introduction and some brief notes on its main features.

A Sample Secondary Source: Reading Journal Article Introductions

Many histories of the American 1960s have centered on a dramatic tale of rise and fall. According to this narrative, the decade began with hopeful idealism—symbolized by the student sit-ins, the rhetoric of the Port Huron Statement (founding manifesto of the New Left), and John F. Kennedy's call to service. It reached its apogee in mid-decade with the Mississippi Freedom Summer, the Berkeley Free Speech Movement, and Lyndon Johnson's electoral landslide. Then, in the context of an escalating and bitterly divisive war in Vietnam and growing social dislocation at home, the idealism curdled into disillusionment and despair. The year 1968—which witnessed the assassinations of Martin Luther King and Robert Kennedy, and the riot at the Democratic Party's national convention in Chicago—marks the symbolic end of 'the sixties': with the New Left and civil rights movements in decline and mired in factionalism, the liberal consensus unravelling, and Richard Nixon triumphant. The strains of 'We Shall Overcome' were displaced by cries of 'Burn, Baby, Burn.' When set alongside this 'brash, bruising blockbuster of a decade' with its 'passion, grandeur and tragedy,' the 1970s have often seemed anticlimactic. Historian Bruce Schulman has noted that 'most Americans regard the Seventies as ... eminently forgettable ... an era of bad clothes, bad hair, and bad music impossible to take seriously.'

In recent years scholars have challenged this master narrative and its implicit 'good sixties'/'bad sixties' dichotomy. They have focused on local organizing, broadened out the chronology of 1960s social movements and political developments, and emphasized similarities, rather than differences, between the 1960s and the decades that bookend them. This article explores two protest movements that were prominent during the 1970s—the struggle for gay rights, and the campaigns against the use of busing as a means to effect social desegregation. These movements tend to be analyzed separately and portrayed very differently. The former is often compared with earlier struggles for equal rights on the part of America's oppressed, and seen as drawing on the radical political tradition that emerged during the 1960s. The anti-busing schedule, in contrast, is usually viewed as symbolizing the new politics of 'backlash,' exemplifying the strength of conservative grassroots organizing that augured the rise of the New Right. Although persuasive, this analysis overlooks significant similarities between the two movements. In important ways anti-busing campaigners drank from the same well of 1960s activism as gay rights protesters, even as they railed against perceived 'excesses' of the so-called 'Age of Aquarius.' Both movements drew on modes of activism, styles of protest, political rhetoric and ideology that were *de rigueur* within 1960s freedom movements. Despite occupying very different positions on the political spectrum, activists in both movements were, each in their own way, children of the 1960s.

Source: Simon Hall, "Protest Movements in the 1970s: The Long 1960s," *Journal of Contemporary History* 43, no. 4 (2008): 665–72. Reprinted here is just the introduction of the article, without footnotes, in order to provide students basic knowledge of the features within this type of writing.

Notes on Journal Article, "Protest Movements in the 1970s: The Long 1960s"—Introduction

Context: *Hall explores the relationship between the 1960s and the 1970s, with the specific goal of understanding the roots of two 1970s protest movements.*

Research Problem:

- *Scholars often describe the 1960s as story of "rise and fall."*
- *"Hopeful idealism," activism, and promise for social change followed by "disillusionment and despair."*
- *The 1970s followed without much fanfare.*
- *Hall questions this broad narrative of 1960s–70s and thinks it's too simplistic. He asks if there could be more continuity between the two decades.*

Thesis: *Despite clear differences in political goals, two 1970s protest movements (struggle for gay rights and campaigns against busing to achieve desegregation) both utilized strategies that originated in the 1960s activists' playbook.*

Evidence: *Not explicitly mentioned here, but suggests archival documents from leaders of both movements (ideological statements; position papers; messaging to followers, etc.). Specific interest in local context & organizing efforts.*

QUESTIONS TO ASK OF SOURCES

Students often copy exactly what they see in secondary sources and neglect to think critically about what they've just written. This is a mistake. After you have finished reading and taking notes on the relevant portions of your book or article, it's time to ask yourself some important questions (make notes on your answers in a different color so that you can keep them distinct from the author's points):

1. *Does the author adequately defend their thesis?* Think about the evidence that the author puts forth to support their argument. Is it enough, or does the thesis go beyond what the evidence actually suggests?

2. *What questions does the author leave unanswered?* If you get to the end of the article or book and have nagging questions, write them down before you forget what they were.
3. *Does the author cite sources that might be helpful to you?* If the author is supporting or disputing another scholar repeatedly in the article or book, chances are that source could be quite useful to your own research. Check the footnotes, endnotes, or bibliography and write down that information.

See Online Companion Exercise 6D
sites.broadviewpress.com/puzzle/chapter-6

CHAPTER 7

Finding Sources and Avoiding Disinformation

In the digital age, we're all responsible for getting to know the university library, its online catalog, and any databases to which your library subscribes. Your library will almost certainly have some tutorials available for students that provide guidance on performing basic and advanced searches. They might be available on the library's website. Alternatively, the library may provide classes designed to help students get acclimated to its holdings and online presence. Most university libraries also provide tours for first-year students, and it's essential that you sign up for one. Lastly, the library's reference personnel are terrific resources and provide students with a much-needed lifeline when they are in the throes of the research process.

Every library catalog is slightly different. While they function in much the same way, enabling students to narrow their search based on author, title, subject, and keyword, their appearance varies. In light of this high degree of variation across institutions, the goal of this chapter is to concentrate on what libraries have in common.

Below, I will highlight WorldCat, an invaluable resource you should be aware of. Then we'll look at some useful strategies for searching for information online, be it through commercial databases owned by your library or through Google. The chapter will end with a discussion of how to determine if a website is reliable for your research project and how to avoid disinformation online.

WorldCat

WorldCat is a network of thousands of library catalogs from across the world. Essentially, when public or university libraries become members of WorldCat, they add their own collection to WorldCat's database. When you search WorldCat as you would a library catalog, you're actually searching thousands of libraries at once. Your search results tell you not only what sources exist, but which libraries actually own them.

WorldCat can be searched from home or from your university library. You will find books, music, and videos, but also digitized primary sources as well as article citations, some of which link to full-text resources that you can download. If you know another language, you might discover resources in other countries that may be relevant to your project. In addition, you can add reviews of sources on WorldCat, which also has an online "Ask a Librarian" feature.

I think of WorldCat as a great first step in seeing what's out there. You may not be able to access everything that comes up in your search, but you'll get a sense of a broader array of resources than you would have seen otherwise.

Finding Sources in Your Library's Databases[1]

Your university library subscribes to some commercial databases, which are extremely useful resources for researchers on all topics and in all disciplines. And if the library divides them by discipline, you may be able to see which databases apply to History. Again, you'll need to consult your library's homepage for instructions. Luckily, some search strategies apply to most commercial databases. Here are some of the most common ones.

Use Boolean operators to focus, broaden, or narrow a search. When you enter your search terms, you'll use the operators AND, OR, and NOT. (These words don't actually need to be capitalized when you do your search, but I am doing so here to distinguish them easily from the surrounding text.) These terms enable you to target the appropriate topic or subject area more efficiently and to leave out unwanted results.

---

1 "Database Search Tips: Overview," MIT Libraries, accessed January 5, 2025, https://libguides.mit.edu/database-search.

- *Use of AND*. When searching in databases, use AND to indicate how your terms should appear in matching results. Let's say, for instance, that I'm doing research on common symptoms of childhood depression. When I do my search, it would be best for me to enter *childhood depression* AND *common symptoms*.

  If you enter the terms without putting in AND, the default for most databases (including Google) is to place an AND after every search term entered. The problem with this is that those words could be located anywhere in the documents found. If you enter *childhood depression common symptoms*, for instance, it could find "childhood" in the title, "depression" in the middle of the document, and "symptoms" at the end. Maybe "common" is used as an adjective five times throughout the piece. Obviously, this won't be very helpful to you when you are looking for useful sources.

- *Use of OR*. In a database search, OR does not function as either/or. It actually tells the database that *at least* one of the terms must come up, and all are permitted. If we go back to our earlier example of *childhood depression common symptoms*, let's say you're unsure if you're going to study depression or anxiety. To find articles that address both of these conditions, you'd enter *depression OR anxiety*.

  The operator OR is also helpful if you are not sure precisely how to refer to a historical topic—or if multiple terms were used for your topic at the time. Suppose you are studying the urban riots of the 1960s. You're not sure if they're called riots, protests, or disturbances, as you've read articles that appear to use these terms interchangeably. In order to make sure your search yields all potential results, you should type the following: *riots OR protests OR disturbances*.

  Databases usually consider AND before OR. It is a good idea to put the words that fall into the OR command in parentheses: *childhood (depression OR anxiety) AND common symptoms*.

- *Use of NOT*. Sometimes, words that you are using automatically trigger the database to bring up results that are not useful to you. If you find that you keep getting results that are not related to your topic, NOT is a good term to employ. For instance, if I were studying the Renaissance of early modern Europe but kept finding articles on the Harlem Renaissance of the 1920s, I might enter *Renaissance NOT Harlem.*

Truncation. It's often the case that searches could employ multiple forms of a word. If you were studying protests during the Civil Rights Movement, you might want to look up "protests," but also "protestors" and maybe even "protesting." Truncation is a search technique that allows you to find multiple forms of a word by employing the appropriate symbol at the end of the word. A common symbol is an asterisk (*). You'd then enter protest* to allow any form of the word to be searched. Other frequently used truncation symbols include !, ?, and #.

A related technique is the use of "wildcards." You can insert a symbol (*) in place of a particular letter when there are multiple spellings of one word. Examples include *hum*r* (for humor or humour) or *recogni*e* (for recognize or recognise).

Search by subject headings. Each database groups topics under particular subject headings, which are *not* intuitive. As a result, when you are starting to search for sources for your paper, you probably won't know what those subject headings are. The easiest way to find appropriate subject headings is to start with a keyword search using what you know to be relevant search terms for your topic. Find one or two sources that you think will be useful. When you click on the data provided for each source, look for the subjects the database assigned to each source. Write those down for future reference, and then search with those terms, exactly as written.

Subject headings are also useful when you are looking for materials in your library's online catalog. If you find one useful book as a source for your paper, search the bibliographic entry for subject headings associated with that book. If you click on one, you will be searching your library's collection for other materials that are listed under that heading.

Database fields. Library databases divide bibliographical data on each source into fields, such as author, title, abstract, publisher, etc. If you confine your search to particular fields (usually accessed by a drop-down box or menu) you can divide your sources in some helpful ways. Here are some examples:

- *Search by author.* Let's say you're trying to access all sources written by a particular author. In that case, you'd want to confine your search to the author field only. If the author is the historical figure you are investigating, then you'd be finding all the primary sources written by that particular individual that are held in that database. Again, this strategy also works when searching in your library's catalog. You can simply search by the "author" field, and you'll find memoirs, speeches, or other sources written by your subject.

- *Search by publication date.* Imagine you are searching for newspaper articles that were written about a particular event, and you had a specific timeframe in mind. If you were investigating the assassination of Martin Luther King, Jr., for instance, you may want to confine your search to April 1968. By limiting your date field, you could avoid newspaper articles not relevant to this topic.

  Students often ignore dates of publication on secondary sources and choose to use articles written much too close to a historical event to be considered authoritative. You can limit the date of publication on a secondary source search in order to avoid this problem. If you were studying the Vietnam War, you'd want to avoid using secondary sources written before 2000 or so. See pp. 67–68 for more on the importance of currency.

Proximity operators. Another way of limiting the number of entries yielded is through proximity operators, which essentially help you to look for two words close to one another in a source, but not necessarily in the same phrase. Two examples of proximity operators are w# and n#:

- *w# = with.* If you entered *abnormal w4 psychology*, you would be saying that 4 words could appear in between *abnormal* and *psychology*, with *abnormal* appearing first. The same order must be maintained as specified by the original search terms.
- *n# = near.* On the other hand, n# indicates that words need to appear near each other but not necessarily in the order you specify. If you said *animal n3 rights*, you might turn up "rights of animals," "animal rights," "rights of endangered animals," and so forth. There would be no more than three words between "animal" and "rights."

Evaluating Websites and Avoiding Disinformation

If excellent resources for historical research are abundant on the internet, you can also come across a great many faulty, misleading, or downright malicious resources online—and it is not always easy to distinguish the former from the latter. In particular, *disinformation*—false or misleading information disseminated with the intent of deceiving or exploiting others or of advancing a particular agenda—abounds on the internet and in social media.

Even individuals with advanced academic credentials can be misled. One 2017 study of the internet research skills of both undergraduate students and history PhDs found that most of the students and also many of the historians failed to identify warning signs of disinformation in the websites they were asked to evaluate. One example was the site minimumwage.com, which featured an article on the problems that would supposedly be caused by raising wages. It turns out that article was produced by a public relations firm that advocates for the restaurant and hotel industries.[2] Fortunately, a wealth of research now exists on how to avoid falling prey to disinformation. The practices this research recommends are simple—if sometimes a little counterintuitive—to implement. Some of these recommended practices are outlined below. Becoming adept at these skills will benefit you far beyond the history classroom.[3]

Stop. When conducting an internet search, the first thing many of us do is immediately click the first results that Google brings up. After all, if they're at the top of the results list, that must mean that they are the best, most pertinent, or most useful sources, right? Unfortunately, this is not always the case; Google's algorithm is easy to game, and plunging right in with the first results it tosses out can all too easily send you down rabbit holes that will be distracting at best, and misleading or deceiving at worst. Instead, once you've run your search, *stop*: don't immediately start clicking the first results. Take some time to scroll down to the bottom of the results page, scanning the titles of the results—and, even more usefully, their URLs and the short abstracts that appear under them—in order to see which of them seem most reliable and most worth your time. Scholars of digital information literacy call this exercising "click restraint."

One key thing to look for when scanning search results and determining what to click on are domain names. You should generally prioritize websites

2 Sam Wineburg and Sarah McGrew, "Lateral Reading: Reading Less and Learning More When Evaluating Digital Information," *Teachers College Record* 121 (2019): 21, https://papers.ssrn.com/sol3/papers.cfm?abstract_id=3048994.

3 The following recommendations are based on the first three steps of Mike Caulfield's four-step "SIFT" method for avoiding online disinformation and improving media literacy. See Mike Caulfield, "SIFT (The Four Moves)," Hapgood, June 19, 2019, https://hapgood.us/2019/06/19/sift-the-four-moves/.

with .edu and .gov domain names, as these are restricted to academic institutions and government entities, respectively. In other words, not just anyone can publish content on .edu and .gov websites, so you can trust that the information they contain is authoritative. The other common internet domain names—.com, .net, and .org—are a mixed bag: they are unrestricted, so anyone can purchase one, and you will thus need to be more careful about evaluating content on them. Be particularly careful with .org domain names: the "organization" label lends them an aura of authority akin to .edu and .gov domains, but in fact it is just as easy to acquire a .org domain name, and consequently to publish disinformation under its cover, as a .com or a .net.

After you've scanned through your search results to determine which will be worthy of closer investigation, you can, and should, ignore the others. Indeed, "critical ignoring"—as Sam Wineburg, another of the foremost scholars studying internet informational literacy, has termed it—is a key skill to master when researching online, alongside its more traditional peers, critical reading and critical thinking. In Wineburg's words, "on the web, where a witches' brew of advertisers, lobbyists, conspiracy theorists and foreign governments conspire to hijack attention, ... critical ignoring is just as important as critical thinking."[4] Tune out the calls of the less reliable sources in your search results, however alluring or provocative their siren songs may be, and focus on those that look like they will be most reputable and most worth your time.

Use "lateral reading" to investigate the source. Before you start reading and taking notes on a website that you have decided seems worth looking into more closely, you need to assess that site's credibility. The most straightforward way to do this might seem to be to investigate the site itself: read its "About" page to get a sense of its background, perspective, and agenda; click through its menu and some of its pages to see how professionally designed it is and how easy it is to navigate; skim some of its articles to determine how up-to-date, well written, and well documented they are, and so forth. For a long time, the standard advice on evaluating online content recommended doing all of these things, and you'll still find versions of this advice today. Yet according to the latest research, investigating a website by exploring the site itself is exactly what you should *not* do.

4 "To Navigate the Dangers of the Web, You Need Critical Thinking—but Also Critical Ignoring," *The Conversation*, May 14, 2021, https://theconversation.com/to-navigate-the-dangers-of-the-web-you-need-critical-thinking-but-also-critical-ignoring-158617.

This advice can seem counterintuitive, because it goes against what most of us are taught to do when evaluating a text (particularly in history courses!), which is to read the text closely and thoroughly, from beginning to end, and to think carefully about it before judging its credibility. On the internet, however, it is very easy for websites pushing disinformation to adopt a convincing veneer of credibility: a .org domain name, high-quality design, an authoritative-sounding "About" page, up-to-date references to scholarly studies, contributors who are specialists with advanced degrees, and all the rest of it.

One example frequently given in scholarship on internet disinformation is the American College of Pediatricians, an organization with a name, and a .org website, that projects neutral, scientific objectivity but which actually advocates anti-LGBT and anti-abortion political positions and has been listed as a hate group by the Southern Poverty Law Center. Without going behind the scenes to find out more about who runs it and what their agenda is, readers who engage too closely for too long with such a website can run the risk of accepting what it says as legitimate. In the 2017 study referred to above (see p. 84), a majority of students who were asked to evaluate an article published on the website of the American College of Pediatricians ended up doing precisely this.[5]

Instead of reading an unfamiliar website "vertically"—that is, staying on the site and combing through it in detail—specialists in digital informational literacy now recommend reading "laterally": leaving the unfamiliar site, opening a new browser tab (or tabs), and searching for reliable background information about the site and its creators. This practice, known as lateral reading, is common among professional fact-checkers, who routinely cross-check information across multiple sites in order to assess whether something they are reading is credible. Only after they've looked into who is behind an unfamiliar site and checked and cross-referenced its claims through lateral searches do they return to the site and continue reading it in detail. According to one 2022 study, learning lateral reading nearly doubled students' ability to evaluate the credibility of online content.[6]

A few easy techniques and resources can be a great help to you as you investigate websites using lateral reading:

5 Wineburg and McGrew, "Lateral Reading," 9–20.

6 Youki Terada, "What Fact-Checkers Know about Media Literacy—and Students Should, Too," Edutopia, May 26, 2022, www.edutopia.org/article/what-fact-checkers-know-about-media-literacy-and-students-should-too.

- *Web search a domain.* Running a basic Google search for the name of the website you are trying to investigate will likely be of minimal value, since it will mainly return lots of pages from the very website you are investigating. Instead, you can use the following special search syntax to look for all references *to* a website that do not come from the site itself: <[WEBSITE URL] -site:[WEBSITE URL]>. So, for example, if you wanted to search what other websites say about minimumwage.com, you would search Google for <minimumwage.com -site:minimumwage.com>.[7]
- *Check author expertise using Google Scholar.* If an article on a website you're investigating has an identified author or authors (and if it doesn't, that in itself can be a sign that you should be wary about using this site as a source), you can look them up on Google Scholar, Google's specialized search engine for searching scholarly literature. Searching for this person on Google Scholar will enable you to check what else they have published, where and when those publications appeared, and—importantly—how many times other scholars have cited those publications in their own work. If a Google Scholar search of an author's name turns up a record (particularly a recent record) of publication in reputable scholarly venues (peer-reviewed journals or books published by university presses) on the same topic or similar topics as the online piece you are investigating, you can safely use this piece as a source—doubly so if this author's other work has been cited frequently! On the other hand, if this author has only published a few things, years ago, and/or on topics unrelated to the topic at hand, you'll want to proceed with caution. And needless to say, if a website's writer has no track record of scholarly publication at all, you should not plan on using that website as a source for a historical research project.
- *Use fact-checking websites.* There are several excellent fact-checking sites online; Snopes.com is one of the most popular, but consulting PolitiFact.com, FactCheck.org, or *The Washington Post* Fact Checker (among others) is also a great way of determining whether the information and claims you've found on the site

7 Michael A. Caulfield, *Web Literacy for Student Fact Checkers* (Pressbooks, 2017), chap. 18, https://pressbooks.pub/webliteracy/chapter/basic-techniques-domain-searches-source-checks-whois/.

you're evaluating are valid or accurate. Snopes.com has also created a master list of disinformation sites, which it updates on a regular basis. The list tells you what kind of fake stories each website produces.[8]

- *Consult real newspapers and news websites.* Institutions such as the *New York Times*, the *Washington Post*, the *Los Angeles Times*, and the *Wall Street Journal* must fact-check everything they publish. It's one of the reasons that they've been around for so long. When it comes to current affairs in particular, if you can't find corroboration for a given claim through at least one such major news outlet, it's a safe bet that the claim is disinformation. If a story is trustworthy and accurate, you should be able to find it in a variety of news sites. Make sure that it's not made up by seeing if you can find it on multiple news sites in the same format.

Find better coverage. Say you are researching African American participation in the Civil War and you find a website claiming that thousands of African Americans fought for the Confederacy. You investigate the site using lateral reading and determine that this claim is dubious. (This, by the way, is something that the author of an actual textbook used in fourth-grade history classes in Virginia was unable to do.[9]) Your task now is to find a source or sources that will offer a well-informed, more impartial, more up-to-date, or otherwise more reliable discussion of the claim and your broader topic. (Spoiler alert: Further research on the topic of African American support for the Confederacy will show that the claims that thousands of Black people fought for the South during the Civil War—claims that are still frequently circulated by Confederate apologists—have absolutely no evidence to back them up.)

Many of the suggestions provided above, including prioritizing .edu and .gov websites and major news organizations, will also help with finding better coverage of a topic. Another helpful resource for finding better coverage—the conventional wisdom of many university faculty members, in particular, notwithstanding—is Wikipedia. Students conducting research are often advised (or required) to steer clear of Wikipedia, on the grounds that "Anyone can edit a Wikipedia entry" and that, as a result, the information

8 Kim LaCapria, "Snopes' Field Guide to Fake News Sites and Hoax Purveyors," Snopes.com, November 2, 2016, www.snopes.com/2016/01/14/fake-news-sites/.

9 See Wineburg and McGrew, "Lateral Reading," 2.

found there has a good chance of being false or misleading. In Wikipedia's early days, the recommendation to avoid it had some merit. Over the years, however, the Wikipedia community has become very good at policing itself and regulating its own editing process, such that the still common claim that anybody can edit a Wikipedia article is itself now beginning to verge on misinformation. As one writer puts it, quoting Sam Wineburg, "Try changing Donald Trump's *Wikipedia* page ... 'Unless you are the highest-badge Wikipedian, you're not going to be able to touch that page.'"[10]

Wikipedia has also adopted strict rules about citing reliable sources in its articles, including clear guidelines about what kinds of sources count as reliable.[11] Because Wikipedia articles are tertiary sources (see above), you still should not cite them in your final paper, but their citations can serve as very helpful ways of finding authoritative sources on a given topic—indeed, many professional fact-checkers use Wikipedia articles exactly this way.[12] For example, the "Confederate Army" subsection of the Wikipedia article on "Military history of African Americans in the American Civil War" includes references to a number of first-rate monographs and other reputable scholarly sources on the topic, including *Searching for Black Confederates: The Civil War's Most Persistent Myth*, a book by the historian Kevin M. Levin published in 2019 by University of North Carolina Press.[13] In short, when you are looking for better coverage of your research topic than you've been able to find so far on the web, or when you are just stuck and don't know where else to go looking for reliable sources, Wikipedia is a great place to start—don't let anybody tell you otherwise! (I should emphasize, though, that it is a great place to *start*. Don't rely on—and certainly don't cite—the Wikipedia article(s) on your topic; instead, follow the article's citations, which will in most cases lead you to the kind of primary and peer-reviewed secondary sources you can find through your library.)

---

10 Terada, "What Fact-Checkers Know about Media Literacy."

11 See https://en.wikipedia.org/wiki/Wikipedia:Verifiability#Reliable_sources.

12 Terada, "What Fact-Checkers Know about Media Literacy."

13 Accessed August 19, 2024, https://en.wikipedia.org/wiki/Military_history_of_African_Americans_in_the_American_Civil_War#Confederate_Army.

CHAPTER 8

Constructing a Thesis Statement

Remember back in Chapter 5, when we talked about your research question? Since then, we have taken a bit of a detour through the world of evidence. The goal of Chapters 6 and 7 was to help you find and evaluate primary and secondary sources so you could begin formulating an answer to the research question. That answer will become the thesis statement, the main argument that will drive every part of your paper from beginning to end. If your thesis does not properly answer your research question, you'll end up with passages in your essay that seem disconnected from the main idea. In fact, you'll probably lose sight of the main idea altogether.

Your thesis statement is best determined in coordination with the research question and the sources you've found. What you'll be doing, essentially, is tinkering with each of these three elements until you have a structure that fits together logically. Frequently, students I taught seem to have learned about thesis statements as if they existed in a vacuum. They talked about the thesis statement in a way that divorced it from the research itself. Often, I found, this was the case because students felt compelled to arrive at a thesis first, and then figure out how to prove it later. They then felt pressured to only select the sources that prove an argument that has prematurely been established as "fact."

In this chapter, we'll discuss the attributes of good thesis statements and consider how some of these attributes—as we'd expect—relate directly to the qualities of good research questions discussed in Chapter 5. We'll then look at an example of how the research question and source material work together in helping us figure out what our thesis needs to say. Lastly, we'll examine a few examples of strong thesis statements. If you would like more practice in evaluating thesis statements, you can find exercises on the book's companion website.

Qualities of a Good Thesis Statement

A good thesis statement can be argued, or is contestable. You might remember that the first attribute of a good research question is that it needs to invite interpretation or analysis. Solid research questions should present tough problems that cannot be resolved with "yes" or "no." It should come as no surprise, then, that the answer to a research question is an argument or debatable statement. The thesis offers one well-reasoned answer to the research question posed.

What do we mean by a debatable statement? Scholars should be able to disagree with it and suggest an alternative understanding or reading that would still make sense. This is why we often talk about a thesis statement as explaining your interpretation of evidence. You are analyzing primary sources and using them to draw your own conclusion about a topic; others might read the same sources and draw different conclusions.

The main thing to remember is that an argument or interpretation is different from a simple statement of fact. If you state a fact that could be confirmed by a Google search in two minutes, or by any high school–level history textbook, then it's not possible to dispute it. Though this may sound like a pretty obvious point, I found that students often had trouble getting past the fact-writing stage of constructing a thesis statement. The less experience students had doing historical research, I discovered, the more difficulty they had writing thesis statements that actually make an argument.

Why do thesis statements so often simply restate facts? Typically, it's because students did not consult enough primary sources. Or they collected primary sources but didn't actually look at them; they might have just listed them in the bibliography in order to fulfill a source requirement. Students generally took this approach because they ran out of time and were scrambling to get their paper written and submitted at the last minute.

It's always going to be easier to simply rehash what another scholar has said about the past. It requires a lot more effort and creativity to find primary sources, analyze them, and figure out how they work together to teach you something new about the past. But this effort is mandatory in order to develop an original interpretation of your sources and an arguable response to your research question. When students merely repeat or restate the interpretations other scholars provide, they produce shallow papers that lack sophistication. They tend to repeat the same basic mantra over and over again, rather than develop an original argument.

A good thesis statement expresses a single main idea as the answer to a research question. At first blush, this criterion looks really obvious. Of course the thesis statement answers the research question posed, right? But this, too, is something that's easier said than done. Again, the problems arise when students cut corners, fail to keep their research question and evidence in mind when crafting a thesis statement, and instead simply rush to get something turned in at the last minute. The thesis statement has something to do with the research question, but does not exactly answer the question posed. Sometimes the reason students falter here is because they start off by trying to tackle more than one issue within their research question (attribute #7; see p. 47). The thesis that results is really confusing.

The end product of this type of mistake is a paper that starts off well—as usually the student has thought a lot about what she is trying to do—but as soon as the thesis appears in the introduction, it doesn't quite make sense. The instructor reading this type of paper feels as if it is two papers in one: the first part is what the student intended to do at the beginning of the assignment, which may take up a page or so, while the second part is a rambling, disjointed attempt to complete the paper, which doesn't quite answer the question posed at the beginning.

A good thesis statement uses specific language. Another frequent problem my students had when they wrote thesis statements is that they employed vague or confusing language. Again, the problem arose because students hadn't quite figured out what they were asking in their research question. If you're not quite sure what question you're trying to answer, it's pretty easy to formulate an argument that lacks precise language.

Clarity takes time to achieve. As they move through the research and writing process, responsible historians—be they students or professionals—expect to sharpen their focus and revise their argument accordingly. This is another reason it is shortsighted to expect the initial wording of your thesis to last through the twists and turns of the research process. As you uncover and evaluate more evidence, your understanding of your sources will deepen accordingly. As a result, your thesis should also become more nuanced and precise.

Students who fail to clarify the language in their thesis statements do themselves an enormous disservice. They make it much harder to write a decent research paper. How can a student expect to craft a clear argument if the core concepts are hazy? If you don't know precisely what you're saying, I guarantee your instructor won't, either! This type of issue is frustrating for university professors, because they spend most of their effort trying to understand what you're saying instead of commenting on the points you're making. Reading a clearly written paper, on the other hand, is enjoyable and intellectually stimulating.

A good thesis is appropriately limited in scope. You might have noticed in Chapter 5 how frequently research questions were either too narrow or too broad in scope. If your question is too narrow, you'll probably have difficulty finding appropriate sources to answer it. It'll be a little bit like trying to find a needle in a haystack. If the sources you've found don't comment on the one issue you're studying, you're stuck. On the other hand, if your question is too broad, then most of the sources you consult appear to answer your research question, and it's quite difficult to determine which ones are best.

How does the problem of scope affect constructing a thesis? As you might expect, if you don't have enough sources, your thesis will rely on very little evidence. For the same reason, it might also be difficult to prove. You will likely fall into the trap of relying on one source repeatedly, perhaps losing sight of its limitations. If, on the other hand, you have too many sources, you will be tempted to make a generalization in your thesis in order to accommodate a broad range of evidence. Since historical writing needs to be precise, this strategy won't work. You will set out to prove more than is reasonable in the space of a short research paper.

A very good way to recognize the importance of limited scope in historical writing is to read other historians' peer-reviewed work. You will see that responsible historians proceed with the utmost caution, only making a claim that they have evidence to support. When they discover that their original plan is either too narrow or too broad in scope, they go back and revise their introduction so that it makes sense in light of their newly updated research agenda.

A good thesis provides a roadmap for the paper. Thus far, our criteria have related the thesis statement directly to attributes of the research question. This criterion is a bit different, because it suggests the purpose that the thesis alone can serve. Well-written thesis statements provide guidance for what is to come in the body of the paper. They tell your reader what to expect in terms of the development of your main ideas. Since historical writing relies heavily on the introduction to spell out the paper's intellectual contribution, the thesis has a big job to do.

It's worth considering what happens when a thesis does not serve as a roadmap. The entire paper crumbles, like a building with no foundation to support it. It meanders with no visible goal, suggesting that it is up to readers to decipher the writer's objective.

Five Characteristics of Strong Thesis Statements

1. A good thesis can be contested or debated.
2. A good thesis expresses a single main idea in response to the research question.
3. A good thesis utilizes specific language.
4. A good thesis is limited in scope.
5. A good thesis provides a roadmap for the paper.

Solving the Puzzle: Research Question, Evidence, and Thesis Statement

How do you actually write the thesis statement? Every paper is different, and there are many guides you can find online that offer tips for wording your thesis statement. The most important thing to remember when starting out is that your research question (RQ), evidence, and thesis statement (TS) have to work in concert to accomplish one goal: formulating a cohesive, focused argument. Let's look at a hypothetical case of how this process might play out.

Evaluate the research question carefully. I start with the following RQ: "How did the John F. Kennedy administration respond to the growing demands of Civil Rights leaders?" This research question gives me a clear focus: the federal government's response to Civil Rights activists during John F. Kennedy's presidency. But the Kennedy administration was in place from January 20, 1961 to November 22, 1963 (the date of his assassination). Civil Rights leaders made demands pretty consistently in that time frame. I have way too many primary sources available to me.

Narrow the question to reflect a shorter chronological scope. "How did the Kennedy administration respond to the growing demands of Civil Rights leaders in 1963?" I've narrowed this framework significantly. Now, though, I'm not sure which set of documents to look at from the year 1963: I have private letters from multiple leaders; formal speeches by Kennedy and members of his administration; newspaper articles from 1963 at key moments of protest or tension; and speeches by Civil Rights leaders that reflect the type of response they received from administration figures. I also have a lot of photographs and video sources from Civil Rights events that took place in 1963. The sources I have collected also cover a range of events from this year.

Reframe the question to focus on one event in 1963. "How did the Kennedy administration respond to the demands for Civil Rights legislation in 1963?" Now I have something to focus on that became a key area of interest for Kennedy in the last six months of his life. Further investigation tells me that the legislation was initially proposed by Kennedy but then stalled for several months in Congress. Passage of Civil Rights legislation grew especially urgent, from President Johnson's perspective, after Kennedy's assassination.

Reframe the question to reflect a focus on the fate of the legislation between June and December 1963. "How did the federal government respond to demands for Civil Rights legislation between June and December 1963?" This revised question appears to provide the appropriate scope for my project. By saying "federal government," I can discuss the executive or legislative branches. The second half of the year helps me deal with the time frame in which most events took place on the topic of proposed Civil Rights legislation.

Keep primary and secondary sources that are directly relevant. I want to start with Kennedy's initial speech about Civil Rights legislation given on June 11, 1963. I want to look for newspaper articles and video clips, as well as internal correspondence that might have been exchanged between members of Congress. Civil Rights leaders' responses to the federal government in the summer of 1963 might tell us a little bit about their impressions of what was happening, too. I will evaluate secondary sources such as biographies of Kennedy and Johnson, as well as political histories of the 1960s. I should also look for scholarly works on the Civil Rights era.

I will use this new set of documents to construct my thesis. My sources show that Kennedy strongly desired Civil Rights legislation but that some members of the House of Representatives were determined to block it. That's my initial hunch, but is there more beneath the surface that explains the delay in getting the legislation to a vote? Why did Kennedy's assassination provide renewed momentum for Johnson? I decide to go back to my sources to see if they can shed light on the internal dynamics behind this issue.

Evaluating Thesis Statements

Consider some examples of *strong* thesis statements below.

- Example 1.

RQ: Why was Eleanor Roosevelt an innovative public figure as First Lady?

TS: "Eleanor Roosevelt recreated the role of the First Lady by her active political leadership in the Democratic Party, by lobbying for national legislation, and by fostering women's leadership in the Democratic Party."[1]

Why it works: Though the three-part structure of this thesis suggests a list, it still holds together because the three ideas support the notion that Roosevelt *recreated the role of First Lady*. That is a focused, specific, and arguable idea. I would expect that in order to make this argument, the writer would need to begin her discussion by explaining what the traditional role of the First Lady was prior to 1933, when Roosevelt became First Lady. They would then proceed to discuss the three items listed in the thesis.

- Example 2.

RQ: How did the American Revolution affect the status of American women?

TS: "While the Revolution presented women [with] unprecedented opportunities to participate in protest movements and manage their family's farms and businesses, it ultimately did not offer lasting political change, excluding women from the right to vote and serve in office."[2]

Why it works: This thesis is specific and provides a precise roadmap for the paper. We know that the writer will start by describing the ways in which the Revolution promised exciting change for women in terms of occupational opportunity, but will then explain that this potential is less significant than political equality. The writer is clearly taking a stand that could be debated.

---

1 For this thesis and its development, see "Argumentation," University of Iowa History Writing Center, accessed January 5, 2025, https://history.uiowa.edu/resources/history-writing-center/writing-guides/argumentation. I have rephrased the research question used in the initial prompt.

2 "Thesis Statements," UCLA Department of History, accessed January 5, 2025, https://history.ucla.edu/thesis-statements/. I have reframed the research question used in the initial prompt.

- Example 3.

RQ: How did the American Revolution affect the status of American women?

TS: "The Revolution had a positive impact on women because it ushered in improvements in female education, legal standing, and economic opportunity. Progress in these three areas gave women the tools they needed to carve out lives beyond the home, laying the foundation for the cohesive feminist movement that would emerge in the mid-nineteenth century."[3]

Why it works: This thesis is quite specific. It is the most provocative in its argument that the Revolution's innovations for women prepared the groundwork for early feminists. While I believe it could be made more cohesive, I would praise this student's careful thinking.

If you would like more practice distinguishing strong thesis statements from weak ones, see the Online Companion Exercise for this chapter.

See Online Companion Exercise 8
sites.broadviewpress.com/puzzle/chapter-8

Quick Tips for Improving Your Own Thesis Statements

1. Begin to identify and highlight thesis statements when you read them in secondary sources. You should be doing this anyway (see Chapter 6), but take note of how published authors structure their thesis statements.
2. With each new iteration of your own thesis statement, ask yourself how you would argue against it. If you can't find a way to do so, then you don't yet have an argument.
3. Look at your thesis statement and your research question and nothing else. Does it answer your question?
4. Share your research question and thesis statement with a friend or family member. What words or concepts are unclear?
5. Look ahead to the writing of your paper. How does the thesis statement suggest your argument should be structured?

3 "Thesis Statements," UCLA Department of History.

CHAPTER 9

Acknowledging Contrary Voices

You've just figured out how to connect your thesis to your research question, and you've even started to separate the relevant evidence from what doesn't belong in your paper. Maybe you've even returned some books to the library, and are really getting a sense of where your paper is going. All great progress! But you still have one last step before you can start working on organizing your ideas: you have to acknowledge those who disagree with you and make space for them at a few points in your paper.

All too frequently, students forget to take this very important step. They learn to prove a point, and stop once they've made their case. They may cite secondary sources that help to back up their argument, but they tend to disregard the others. Academic writing requires that you learn to break out of this rigid formula.

Here's why. Academic writing operates on a specific set of assumptions. Like scholars in other disciplines, historians view themselves as building on the work of others, and as offering viewpoints that differ from those of others. Remember when we surveyed strategies for reading journal articles in Chapter 6? You should recall that in their introductions, historians explain how they position themselves intellectually vis-à-vis other historians. (See p. 75.) You need to do that too.

Don't get scared; it's not as hard as it sounds. As a new student of history, you're not expected to have footnotes that span paragraphs. After briefly researching a topic, you won't have the expertise that would come with years of study and preparation necessary for a PhD. But you should have a very basic sense of where you might agree and disagree with others who have written on the same basic topic. That much comes from having read a couple of secondary sources. Or, when interpreting primary sources, you should be able to anticipate perspectives that differ from your own. In those circumstances, you can simply acknowledge alternative ways of reading the same text that you can infer from your own careful analysis.

Here is another helpful way to think about it. Academic writing ultimately works best when authors imagine themselves to be in *conversation* with other thinkers. One of the most important books on this topic is *They Say/I Say: The Moves that Matter in Academic Writing.*[1] As the title suggests, the authors' goal is to illustrate how academic writing actually resembles an intellectual conversation: "For us, the underlying structure of effective academic writing—and of responsible public discourse—resides not just in stating your own ideas, but in listening closely to those around us, summarizing their views in a way that they will recognize, and responding with our own ideas in kind."[2] Just as we try to follow certain rules when listening to someone talk, we follow much the same pattern in academic writing. We have a keen understanding not just of our own perspective, but of those who have already spoken on the topic. We may have even formed our own point of view, in part, as a response to what others said before us. *They Say/I Say* provides practical advice for writing with others' ideas in mind, and is a terrific resource for this aspect of paper writing for students in all disciplines (not just History). It presents templates that students can use to help them frame their own ideas in relation to a larger scholarly discussion on a topic.

This chapter provides some tips as you begin to conceive of your own writing in this light. If this is your first time writing a historical research paper, please don't expect to make this transition overnight. It takes a lot of experience writing research (or argumentative) papers to build up your confidence. So, keep your expectations realistic. But also recognize that a little bit of effort can go a long way in adding sophistication to your writing.

1 Gerald Graff and Cathy Birkenstein, *They Say/I Say: The Moves that Matter in Academic Writing,* 2nd ed. (W.W. Norton, 2010). The most recent edition of *They Say/I Say* is the sixth, having been published in 2024.

2 Graff and Birkenstein, *They Say/I Say,* 3.

Why We Acknowledge Other Voices

In academic writing, there are specific reasons why it helps to acknowledge voices that contradict what you're saying. Let's take a look at some of these first, and then delve into some strategies for doing so.

It helps the reader understand why your argument is important. When we frame our own perspective in light of what others have already said on the topic, it demonstrates that what we are saying has broader relevance. It also helps to give it some context. As Graff and Birkenstein explain in *They Say/I Say*, imagine overhearing a heated debate among four of your friends, all of whom felt passionately about a particular topic. If you heard only one person speaking but no one else, you might be able to identify bits and pieces of what that person was saying. But you'd also be really confused as to how that person's ideas related to others', and why she felt the way she did. Now think about how different it would be if you heard two of the voices, and then three, and then four. Once you had heard the entire conversation, your understanding of the topic would expand dramatically. It's the same with writing. You're helping your reader to understand the relevance of your arguments by representing other points of view along the way.[3]

It makes your writing much more engaging. Have you ever listened to a lecture by a professor that was kind of boring? What about a panel discussion where the participants had different viewpoints on an issue you found fascinating? Listening to a conversation about an issue, rather than one person's monologue, can often help to keep an audience much more involved. The same goes with writing. Multiple perspectives add color and depth to your writing. This is especially the case if you are dealing with a well-known or highly controversial topic. Your reader will be happy to see that you're giving a nod to disparate opinions.

You will become a more credible writer. If you write with others' perspectives in mind, you will come across as well-versed on your topic. Again, let's think of an analogous situation. Think of your latest experience watching a news channel. Frequently, experts are called in to provide some perspective on an issue. If the expert evinced little to no familiarity with common viewpoints or debates on the topic, you'd be much less inclined to trust

3 In *They Say/I Say*, pp. 13–14, the authors cite a well-known passage by philosopher Kenneth Burke, who compared academic debate to ongoing conversation at a party. The person entering the conversation is said to "put in [their] oar." This example is intended to convey the same basic message.

their opinion than if the opposite were the case. The same is true with academic writing.[4]

You get to defend your own viewpoints, rather than just present them. Defending your own opinion requires you to think a bit differently about your topic than you would if you were just presenting an argument and offering evidence to support it. When challenged with counterarguments, you're forced to think about why your own perspective makes more sense than the alternatives. It's a great thought exercise. If you've served on your high school mock trial or debate team, or observed a competition, you may have noticed that participants have to practice by preparing arguments on both sides of an issue. Doing so enables them to sharpen their argumentative skills. Presenting counterarguments to your thesis within your paper will help you make an even stronger case for your own thinking on an issue.[5]

Ground Rules for Representing Other Opinions in Your Paper

Become fully aware of arguments different from your own. One of the main reasons students fail to acknowledge contrasting viewpoints is because they don't look for them when doing research. It's important to take notes on sources that complicate, or even contradict, the perspective represented in your developing thesis, even if it feels awkward at first. It's easier to ignore these sources, of course, because they challenge us to think in ways we're not used to. They might even cause us to revise the thesis statement a bit.

In order to incorporate contrary voices into your argument, it is important to start noting what they're saying. One way you can do this easily is to simply put those notes in a different color or font. If you think of a way to refute viewpoints while taking your notes, by all means include those thoughts in your own research notes. But distinguish them somehow so that you know they're *your* thoughts, not those of another author. If you find primary sources that appear to disprove or complicate your thesis, you may want to consider adding some nuance to the body of your paper that shows that you are familiar with those sources.

4 "The Power of Opposing Views: Integrating Naysayers in Your Essay," Gilliam Writers Group, accessed January 5, 2025, www.gilliamwritersgroup.com.

5 "The Power of Opposing Views," Gilliam Writers Group.

Represent the viewpoint accurately. It's important to make sure you fully understand the source first. In order to do so, read the author's argument a few times and try to adopt their perspective. If you misrepresent the other person's argument, then you lose credibility as a writer. You also risk confusing your reader because your own perspective may come across as muddled and unpersuasive.

Do not use condescending language. Present the alternative opinion using language that does not reflect pre-judgment. Once you've presented it fairly, then you can explain, in a balanced tone, why you believe it is an incorrect or weak position compared to your own.

Strategies for Introducing Contrary Voices

Quote the opposition, and then refute that point. As you'll see in the chapter on quotations (Chapter 14), these should be used selectively and sparingly. However, should you choose to quote a source and then refute it, make certain that you have chosen the most critical passage and that it is not too long. If you leave a portion of the quotation out, make sure that the omitted portion does not change the author's intended meaning. Students frequently make the mistake of quoting much more than is necessary to convey the main idea of a passage. Once you have shared the quote, briefly summarize the main idea of the quotation in your own words, and then refute it.

To introduce your quotation, you'll want to make sure it's clear to your reader, either in the text or the footnotes, that you are referring to someone else's views rather than your own. Then, choose a neutral verb to frame the quotation, such as "contends," "argues," or "maintains."

Paraphrase the opposition, and then point out flaws in the argument. Most often, paraphrasing is the best choice. Since you would not be using a direct quotation, though, do make sure you have an accurate understanding of your source. The same neutral verbs apply in paraphrased writing as in quotations. You would then explain your points of disagreement.

Offer a concession, but then explain the limitations of the viewpoint. In this scenario, you begin by acknowledging that the alternative viewpoint has some merit. It might be the case that you don't even use the author's name in the text, but allow that the perspective is a valid one. Concessions might begin "Granted, it is true that ..." or "While some may fairly point out that ..." Then, you'll follow up by explaining why your point outweighs the merits of the alternative: "But despite that scenario, point X would be the case most of the time."

Pose a rhetorical example. This strategy involves adopting your reader's perspective and trying to anticipate the point in your argument that she might be most likely to disagree with or raise an objection to. You step out of the comfort zone of presenting your argument and say, "But what if this were the case?" Then you get to explain why your argument is still valid.

Acknowledging Contrary Voices in Practice

The templates in *They Say/I Say* offer plenty of examples of how to incorporate opposing views into your writing. Rather than reprint those here, I am doing something a bit different. On the next few pages, you'll see selections from Martin Luther King, Jr.'s *Letter from Birmingham Jail* from April 1963, one of the finest primary source examples of this type of writing. King wrote with the viewpoints of his critics in mind, and addressed them using a number of rhetorical strategies throughout the document. I'm highlighting passages that illustrate King's nods to contrary voices. Beneath the text samples, I've explained what he does and why it works as an argumentative device.

By including King's famous letter, I'm introducing you to one of the finest examples we have of writing that keeps other perspectives in mind. Reading this type of primary source jolts me into a new frame of mind. By having King in the back of my head, I begin to see my own academic writing as part of a larger debate. Hopefully, you will too.

Strategies for Acknowledging Contrary Voices

1. Quote opposition and then refute the point.
2. Paraphrase the opposition, and then point out flaws in the argument.
3. Offer concession, then explain limitations of viewpoint.
4. Pose rhetorical example, then refute that perspective.

16 April 1963
My Dear Fellow Clergymen:

While confined here in the Birmingham city jail, I came across your recent statement calling my present activities "unwise and untimely." ❶ Seldom do I pause to answer criticism of my work and ideas. If I sought to answer all the criticisms that cross my desk, my secretaries would have little time for anything other than such correspondence in the course of the day, and I would have no time for constructive work. But since I feel that you are men of genuine good will and that your criticisms are sincerely set forth, I want to try to answer your statement in what I hope will be patient and reasonable terms. ❷

I think I should indicate why I am here in Birmingham, since you have been influenced by the view which argues against "outsiders coming in." ❸ I have the honor of serving as president of the Southern Christian Leadership Conference, an organization operating in every southern state, with headquarters in Atlanta, Georgia. We have some eighty-five affiliated organizations across the South, and one of them is the Alabama Christian Movement for Human Rights. Frequently we share staff, educational and financial resources with our affiliates. Several months ago the affiliate here in Birmingham asked us to be on call to engage in a nonviolent direct action program if such were deemed necessary. We readily consented, and when the hour came we lived up to our promise. So I, along with several members of my staff, am here because I was invited here. I am here because I have organizational ties here.... ❹

You deplore the demonstrations taking place in Birmingham. But your statement, I am sorry to say, fails to express a similar concern for the conditions that brought about the demonstrations. ❺ I am sure that none of you would want to rest content with the superficial kind of social analysis that deals merely with effects and does not grapple with underlying causes. It is unfortunate that demonstrations are taking place in Birmingham, but it is even more unfortunate that the city's white power structure left the Negro community with no alternative.... ❻

You may well ask: "Why direct action? Why sit ins, marches and so forth? Isn't negotiation a better path?" You are quite right in calling for negotiation. Indeed, this is the very purpose of direct action. Nonviolent direct action

❶ King quotes the opposition (strategy #1) in the initial sentence of his letter. This illustrates to his readers that he is responding with their perspective in mind.

❷ In the latter portion of this paragraph, King praises the intentions of his critics, avoiding a tone of condescension. He respects his critics despite their differences. By following these key ground rules, King makes it more likely that his critics will read his letter with an open mind.

❸ King notes that his readers have been "influenced" by those who were opposed to "outsiders coming in." This strategy (#1) is interesting. It acknowledges the existence of the different perspective, but entertains the possibility that his readers might not, necessarily, subscribe to it.

❹ King has explained why he is not an outsider in the way that his readers might have assumed. This is the second half of strategy #1 initiated in passage ❸.

❺ King paraphrases his readers' sentiments (strategy #2). He then explains that it doesn't seem quite logical to abhor demonstrations, but to feel no concern for what is causing them. King begins to suggest that his critics are missing the mark by blaming the victim.

❻ King repeats the same strategy utilized in ❺. But this time he is more explicit by naming the parties involved. The only reason protests are taking place is because no other option has been made available to African Americans.

seeks to create such a crisis and foster such a tension that a community which has constantly refused to negotiate is forced to confront the issue. It seeks so to dramatize the issue that it can no longer be ignored. ❼ My citing the creation of tension as part of the work of the nonviolent resister may sound rather shocking. But I must confess that I am not afraid of the word "tension." I have earnestly opposed violent tension, but there is a type of constructive, nonviolent tension which is necessary for growth. Just as Socrates felt that it was necessary to create a tension in the mind so that individuals could rise from the bondage of myths and half truths to the unfettered realm of creative analysis and objective appraisal, so must we see the need for nonviolent gadflies to create the kind of tension in society that will help men rise from the dark depths of prejudice and racism to the majestic heights of understanding and brotherhood. The purpose of our direct action program is to create a situation so crisis packed that it will inevitably open the door to negotiation. I therefore concur with you in your call for negotiation. ❽ Too long has our beloved Southland been bogged down in a tragic effort to live in monologue rather than dialogue....

There comes a time when the cup of endurance runs over, and men are no longer willing to be plunged into the abyss of despair. I hope, sirs, you can understand our legitimate and unavoidable impatience. You express a great deal of anxiety over our willingness to break laws. This is certainly a legitimate concern. Since we so diligently urge people to obey the Supreme Court's decision of 1954 outlawing segregation in the public schools, at first glance it may seem rather paradoxical for us consciously to break laws. ❾ One may well ask: "How can you advocate breaking some laws and obeying others?" The answer lies in the fact that there are two types of laws: just and unjust. I would be the first to advocate obeying just laws. One has not only a legal but a moral responsibility to obey just laws. Conversely, one has a moral responsibility to disobey unjust laws. ❿ I would agree with St. Augustine that "an unjust law is no law at all."

Source: African Studies Center, University of Pennsylvania, accessed March 26, 2025, https://www.africa.upenn.edu/Articles_Gen/Letter_Birmingham.html.[6]

❼ King utilizes strategy #4. He suggests the question that is probably on the minds of his readers—why don't African Americans just negotiate? He explains that negotiation can only happen when both parties agree that it is a necessity. That is the goal of nonviolence.

❽ King suggests that ultimately he and his readers have the same goal—both parties want to negotiate. He spends time outlining what he has in common with his rivals.

❾ King utilizes a combination of strategies #2 and #3. He describes the concern among the clergy regarding the tactics that nonviolent demonstrators have utilized. He acknowledges that it probably seems odd to them that protesters are willing to break laws.

❿ King again utilizes strategy #4. He suggests a paradox that has probably crossed the minds of his critics: Why are the demonstrators willing to respect some laws but not others? He points out that some laws are just and others are not. He believes people are morally bound to disobey unjust laws, in the hope that those laws will be changed.

---

6 King's letter was first written on scraps of paper. Several staff then typed the letter based on his notes. Versions of the letter, which appeared in different publications (starting in May 1963), vary slightly from one another. The rhetorical strategies identified here are not affected by these minor variations in language.

CHAPTER 10

Organizing Your Ideas

Have you read comments like "repetitive" or "confusing" in the margins of your papers? Usually, those types of comments refer to issues of organization that were not resolved early on in the writing process. In my experience, organizational problems are at the heart of most students' struggles with expository writing. I think the reason that organization poses such a distinct challenge for students is that it requires a commitment to clear, logical thinking that comes from having a fresh perspective on your topic. When you get so immersed in the details of your topic that you lose sight of the big picture, it can be really hard to figure out how to organize your ideas.

You can tackle your organizational challenges most effectively by addressing them during the research process—in other words, before you start to write. If you wait until the last minute to think about structure and logic, you'll lack the time and energy to give these tough questions the attention they deserve. The purpose of this chapter is to provide some strategies for organizing your ideas at different stages of the writing process. By setting aside time to see the big picture, you'll help yourself to avoid feeling overwhelmed by the details of your topic.

Visual Organizers

The key to effective organization is your ability to step back from the trees, so to speak, and take a look at the forest, with your research question in mind. Your thesis statement will ultimately guide your paper, of course, but you might still be wrestling with what your evidence is telling you. You might not be sure where you have the strongest evidence and where your argument is considerably weaker. Visual organizers can help resolve some of these questions by helping you see ways to connect your ideas that you hadn't previously considered. Once you have mapped out your evidence, you might find it a lot easier to construct your thesis statement.

Below you'll find three models for brainstorming how your ideas may fit together. By playing around with these models a bit, you may reach a new level of understanding of your topic that eluded you earlier. Recognize, though, that there are plenty of possibilities online of other visual organizers if these don't work out.[1]

1. The first is a Venn diagram, which works well for research topics that compare and contrast two topics. The overlapping portion in the middle provides a summary of what the two topics have in common.
2. The second is a graphic organizer, which is grouped according to subtopics that surround the main topic.
3. The third is simply a series of notes that you pin to a bulletin board. You could also use sticky notes, and then move them around as you contemplate different organizational strategies.

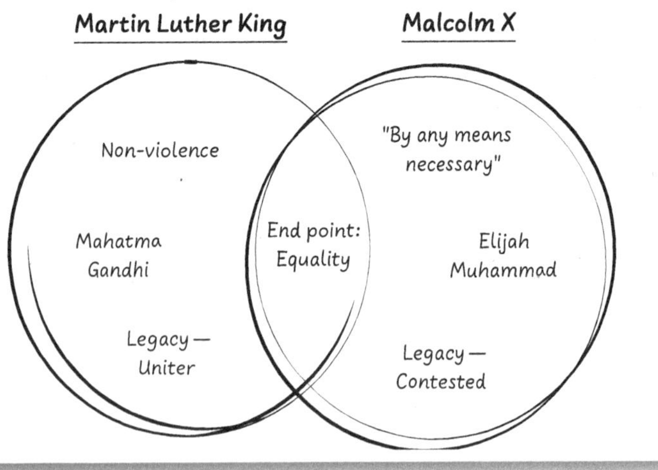

1 See, for example, Miro, Lucidchart, Coggle, FigJam, and Milanote.

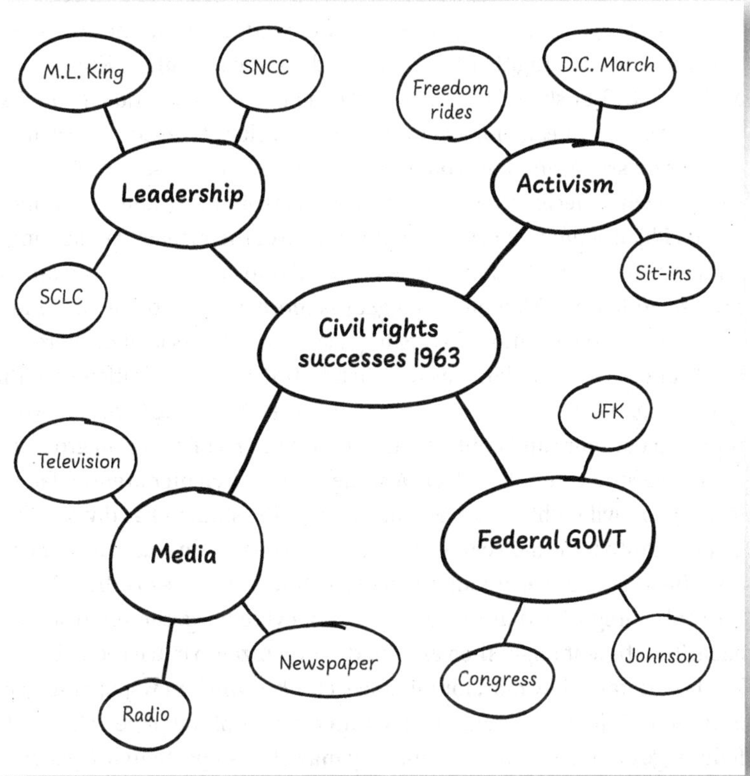

The Presidency of Lyndon B. Johnson — Defining Events

Political Experience
House (1937–49)
Senate (1949–61)
Choice as VP (1961)
Relationship with JFK
Texan in Kennedy Admin.

Presidency (1963)
JFK Assassination
Swearing in/Air Force One
Mood of Country
Legacy of JFK

1964 Campaign
Civil Rights Legislation
Tonkin Gulf Resolution
Goldwater's Challenge
Landslide Victory

1965 Domestic Agenda
Voting Rights Act
Immigration
Education
Great Society
War on Poverty

Vietnam 1966–67
Federal Spending
Deployments
Antiwar Movement
Domestic vs. Foreign Priorities

1968 Discord & Polarization
Tet Offensive
Defeat in NH Primary
Nationwide Protests
Democratic Convention

The first example shows a very simple Venn diagram that is used to contrast the Civil Rights Movement leaders Martin Luther King, Jr. and Malcolm X. They shared the same goal of achieving racial equality but had very different strategies for achieving that goal. They diverged in the content of their message (emphasis on non-violence versus willingness to accept violence when necessary); in their source of inspiration (Mahatma Gandhi versus Elijah Muhammad); and in the nature of their legacy. While King is largely remembered as someone who could find common ground among diverse audiences, Malcolm X's legacy is more contested due to some of the controversial positions he assumed as a Civil Rights leader. There may be other points of similarity as well, in addition to areas of difference. This type of organizer might help a writer when they are trying to decide which topics to compare and contrast, and to find points of common ground.

The second example reflects a student's research on potential factors leading to Civil Rights achievements in 1963. The student has divided their evidence into four main categories, including leadership, activism, media, and the federal government. Each of the four categories is then divided into sub-categories that reflect sources of evidence gathered to support each. The student might then expand this organizer to make room for finer levels of detail. They may, for instance, choose which newspaper articles and television clips to reference within the text of the paper. Or, for the federal government sub-section, they may choose particular legislation passed by Congress, or personal letters or public speeches from either Presidents Kennedy or Johnson. This type of organizer allows students to see where they have strong evidence and where they may need to add further support to an argument.

A third organizer is simply made using a series of sticky notes, each of which contains a list of subheadings describing a particular aspect of Lyndon Johnson's presidency. Here, I have organized the information chronologically, grouping together Johnson's political roles prior to his assumption of the presidency in November 1963. The advantage of this method is that you can easily compare the sections of your paper and regroup as needed if you change your organizational scheme. Should you add details, you could just move the sticky notes around in order to accommodate new information.

A fourth suggestion is to cut and paste some of the text from your notes into a word cloud, which can be created on many different websites such as worditout.com, tagxedo.com, WordArt.com, and wordclouds.com. You will see an image of the words in the text, with the most frequently used words printed largest in the picture. This type of tool may help you locate themes that you may have overlooked in working with your sources thus far.

Once you have finished mapping out your evidence in the graphic organizer you choose, ask yourself the following questions:

- What common themes can you find that help to tie individual categories of evidence together?
- Is there a sense in which a portion of your evidence suggests one thing, and the rest suggests something different? Where do your contrary voices belong in this picture?
- How do contrary arguments cause you to look at your evidence differently? Is there a place where you can add more nuance where before you saw only black and white?

This is the time—when your evidence is mapped out in a different format—to find new relationships and connections you hadn't seen before. This exercise can help you get past the "list thesis" formula and move toward something more sophisticated. Ultimately, you want to see what insights you discover when studying evidence in a new light.

Let's return to two of the examples above. If I were looking at the Civil Rights successes of 1963, I have four categories of evidence. I found that Civil Rights leadership, grassroots activism, media coverage, and federal action all contributed to the success of the Civil Rights Movement. But as we discussed in the example featured in Chapter 8, the federal government dragged its heels on getting legislation passed, even though grassroots activists, the media, and Civil Rights leaders pushed vigorously for social change. My thesis might contain a clause that reflects this difference. Let's say my research question reads, "How did the Civil Rights Movement make strides toward racial equality in 1963?" My thesis might then read, "Despite an inconsistent response by the federal government, Civil Rights leaders and grassroots activists worked with the news media to heighten public awareness of racial inequality in the US in 1963."

Let's also look at the Lyndon Johnson example in the same light. Moving through the Johnson administration chronologically, how would I organize these notes? I might point out that Johnson seemed to accomplish the most domestically between 1963 and 1965. But once the Vietnam conflict had worsened after 1965, his progress was interrupted. I would turn to my biographers of Johnson (secondary sources) to see how they interpret the years of Johnson's presidency. Do they also identify a divide between the years 1963–65 and 1966–68? Or do they periodize his administration differently? Rather than just presenting a simple chronological explanation of Johnson's accomplishments while in office, with this analysis I now work on developing a particular interpretation. In the historical narrative I'm thinking of, 1965 might have been Johnson's peak. I go back to primary and secondary sources and test this hypothesis for additional support. If I find a few differing perspectives on this, then I know I've identified a debatable thesis.

The Purpose of an Outline

Even when you have your thesis in place, it can still be overwhelming to figure out how to put everything together into a cohesive, logical draft. If you have been swimming in a sea of facts and sources, and are feeling pretty nervous about writing the paper itself, I would strongly recommend creating an outline before beginning your draft. In my experience, students who construct an outline prior to writing a paper only stand to benefit from making the effort. The problem I've discovered, however, is that the act of writing an outline is unfamiliar to many students, so they tend to get very frustrated when they try to do so. They might write phrases to represent complex ideas and end up with an outline that is so abbreviated as to be virtually useless. Or, they write an outline that is so detailed that it is almost the same length as the paper. Neither of these strategies, unfortunately, is very helpful.

Let's first review some chief purposes of the outline. From there, we'll look at what every outline should include, and then examine some strategies for how to write one.

An outline requires you to be certain that every idea you articulate relates to the thesis statement and to steer clear of fluff. If you have tried to write a paper at the last minute, you know what it feels like to come up short on pages and have to pad the paper so that it meets the page requirement. This is a problem for any paper, but particularly a research paper that demands a great deal of time and effort. Doing an outline first will help to ensure that you don't find yourself in that situation, because you will know in advance that every sentence relates to the thesis. Most importantly, you'll be able to plan ahead so you don't come up short on pages.

An outline is an organizational tool. Intellectually, most students recognize that doing an outline helps to promote better organization of a paper.

But those whom I have taught often treat the outline as something that they just need to get done in order to fulfill a requirement. In actuality, an outline is a tool that allows us to test out different ways of structuring a paper. Before the outline becomes the blueprint for the paper you're about to write, it provides a structure for experimentation.

An outline helps you to quickly see problems that you might encounter in writing a paper. When you take the time to write an outline, you should be able to detect areas that need improvement. For example, maybe you don't have enough evidence to support one of your points, but way too much to support another. Maybe you have not engaged contrary voices at any point in your paper, and now see a place in your argument when doing so might make a lot of sense. Maybe you are relying exclusively on secondary sources in one spot, but haven't found any primary sources to support your assertion. Or, as is often the case, maybe your paper feels unbalanced. The introduction is way too long in comparison to the rest of the paper. In this sense, the outline can serve a purpose similar to that of the visual organizer.

Formatting an Outline

As you set out to construct an outline, don't lose sight of the most important reason you're taking the time to do this: to make sure that when you write the paper, *you stick to the thesis*. For this reason, when you start writing your outline, put the thesis at the top of the first page. That way you're going to see it every time you refer back to the outline. Whenever you revise the thesis, you should include those revisions on your outline.

OUTLINE SUBDIVISIONS

Your outline should include an introduction, a body, and a conclusion. Proportionally, the body of the outline should be much longer than the introduction and the conclusion.

The *introduction* should establish the historical context; introduce the research question or problem to be addressed; include some reference to the types of evidence used to support the thesis in the essay; and end with the *thesis statement*.

The *body* portion of the outline should include a title for each section. Each section should proceed logically from the argument established in your thesis, developing your thesis in the process. Details in each body segment of the outline should include primary and secondary source evidence that illustrates the precise point you are making in that section. If you have identified specific quotations that you'd like to use in the course of your paper, you can include them in your outline. This is a very good way of making sure that your quotations are appropriately integrated and connected to your argument, and that you are not using them to merely pad your paper. Anything not connected to the thesis should not be included.

The *conclusion* portion of the outline should restate the thesis as a persuasive answer to the research question, given the evidence presented. It should also suggest the broader relevance of the paper itself. Ask yourself why your argument should matter to a reader. How will it alter her understanding of the subject matter?

Sections of the outline are headed by Roman numerals (I, II, and III) and subdivided by letters (A, B, and C). Details under each letter are listed using Arabic numerals (1, 2, 3). Continue for another sublayer of detail with lower case letters (a, b, and c). A good rule of thumb is that you can never have a subdivision with only one layer of detail. For instance, you can't have an A without a B, or a 1 without a 2.

If your goal is primarily to figure out the organization of your argument, don't get too bogged down in the details of how many headings and subheadings you have. Ultimately, you want to create a plan for your paper that makes sense and that keeps you on track when you're writing.

TOPIC OR SENTENCE OUTLINES

Outlines can express ideas in either phrases or full sentences. Topic outlines require each subdivision to contain brief phrases that allude to what that section will discuss. If you are trying to establish the basic order and logical format for arguing your thesis, the topic outline will help you figure out when you plan to talk about each issue. It will also give you a sense of hierarchy: Which ideas might translate well to topic sentences, and which details support them? Topic outlines will be especially useful to you if you are very pressed for time and simply do not have the ability to construct a sentence outline before your paper is due. The limits of topic outlines are significant, however. You can complete one without having done much of the thinking that would be necessary had you written complete sentences.

Provided that you have given yourself enough time to write one, doing a sentence outline will be far more helpful to you in drafting the paper. For a sentence outline, each point of the outline is exactly one sentence. If done properly, reading the outline from start to finish will actually seem like you are reading logically structured topic sentences of your paper. You are essentially making the exact argument that you'll make in the paper, and will later only need to add supporting details from primary and secondary sources. You will also know precisely when you intend to draw upon what sources, and which quotations you plan to use.[2]

Guidelines for Writing an Outline

Since you are starting by putting your thesis statement at the top of the page and using it as your guide, really make sure that your thesis answers your research question, and that it reflects your current thinking regarding your research. Once you have done that, keep these important guidelines in mind.

There is more than one way to structure your paper. Students often forget that they can make an effective argument in a number of different ways. While your thesis should provide a roadmap for the key points you need to make, you should be able to envision a few different ways to put your ideas together. Even if I gave you and your friend the same exact thesis to argue, you could have very different ways of making the same argument. Don't be afraid to sketch out a couple of different possibilities before you construct the entire sentence outline.

Once you arrive at your chosen structure, make sure it develops your thesis in a logical fashion. The key word here is *develops.* A good history paper has ideas that evolve and become more nuanced as the paper goes on; it doesn't just present a simple mantra and keep drumming the same message over and over again into the reader's head. Remember that you're taking your reader on a journey with a beginning, a middle, and an end. If you can rearrange the points you're making in the body section because they are all making the same exact argument in different ways, that's a problem.

Ask questions of the outline. Once you arrive at what you believe to be the optimal structure for your paper, you should question it by asking the following:

- *Does my thesis drive my outline?* Every point you make should be anticipated by your thesis statement. Consider each point

2 See "Four Main Components for Effective Outlines," Purdue Online Writing Lab, accessed March 28, 2025, https://owl.purdue.edu/owl/general_writing/the_writing_process/developing_an_outline/index.html.

individually and ask this question. If the answer is no, then revise accordingly.

- *Am I arguing my thesis thoroughly?* Is there any portion of your thesis that you have not sufficiently addressed?
- *Are you able to orally describe the structure you have formulated?* Get into a room by yourself, close the door, and summarize how you're going to structure your paper. Record yourself on your phone. Let it sit for a day or two, and then listen to your voice recording. Does it make sense? If not, go back and revise.
- *If my argument shifts halfway through the outline, does my thesis anticipate that shift?* Your paper should not present a dramatic surprise to the reader partway through. If you make a point that appears to come out of the blue in the outline, then it needs to be incorporated into the thesis.
- *Have I considered viewpoints that disagree with my thesis?* Make sure your outline includes attention to opposing perspectives, as discussed in Chapter 9.
- *Am I relying too heavily on one source?* An outline provides another opportunity to gauge how much you may be relying on individual sources. Take advantage of the chance to make these revisions before you end up writing an unbalanced paper.[3]

See Online Companion Exercise 10
sites.broadviewpress.com/puzzle/chapter-10

Reverse Outlines

Most students I have taught don't realize that outlines can also be useful after you have written a draft. You can think of a *reverse outline* as a way to verify that the draft you have written is logically structured. Once you have completed your first draft, number each paragraph of your paper. Then write your thesis at the top of a separate sheet of paper and write the corresponding list of numbers under the thesis statement. Next to each

3 "How to Structure and Organize Your Paper," Odegaard Writing and Research Center, accessed March 28, 2025, depts.washington.edu/owrcweb/wordpress/resources/handouts.

number, write a phrase or sentence that summarizes the main point made in that paragraph. Essentially, you have outlined what you have written, in rough form. Here are some questions you should ask yourself once you have completed the reverse outline:

- *Were you able to summarize each of your paragraphs in one sentence?* If the answer is no, then you should go back and check the content of your paragraphs. If you are having difficulty figuring out the single main idea that sums up each paragraph, so will your reader. You may need to break up some paragraphs if they are too lengthy, or reorganize a paragraph that is unfocused.
- *Do the ideas follow in logical order?* See if you can identify a logical progression from one idea to the next. If there is repetition, or a transition that doesn't make sense, you need to go back to the drawing board at that point in your paper.
- *Are there ideas that do not connect to the thesis statement?* Remember that one of the biggest problems students have when writing is veering off course. Make sure that all of your ideas can be anticipated logically from the thesis statement.
- *Have you done what you promised to do in your thesis statement?* Make sure that you have delivered on the promises you made in the introduction.[4]

Use your reverse outline to determine where your draft needs to be edited so it is organized properly. When you have made those changes, do the same exercise again and see if the structure of your paper is more cohesive.

One of the best characteristics of an outline is that it forces you to get to the point of your paper and the basics of its argument—quickly. If you can't do that by the time you start to write, you have some more work to do. If you are unsure of how to fix your outline, try it out on a friend or family member. Use the outline to guide you through an oral summary of your paper. Sometimes, hearing yourself talk about your ideas can help you figure out where your argument comes together nicely, and where it has weaknesses.

---

4 "Reverse Outlining," Monmouth University Tutoring and Writing Services, accessed March 28, 2025, https://www.monmouth.edu/resources-for-writers/documents/reverse-outlining.pdf/.

CHAPTER 11

The Conventions of Historical Writing

Every discipline, be it History, English, Political Science, Anthropology, or Genetics, has its own stylistic conventions. By "stylistic conventions," I mean those writing norms or standards that scholars in the field take for granted as essential within the framework of that discipline. Every time you write a paper in a new field—even if it's the only one you'll ever write!—you should pay attention to the conventions that matter to experts in this field. While your professor certainly doesn't expect you to be a pro in historical writing the minute you pick up your pen or take out your laptop, there are a few key conventions to keep in mind. Some of these conventions apply to a number of different humanities disciplines, but many are specific to History. The purpose of this chapter is to explain the most important conventions associated with historical writing so that when you go to write your research paper, you start off on the right foot.

Content Conventions

One of the most efficient ways to determine what matters to historians is to look carefully at the comments that instructors often write on students' history papers.[1] Here are some to keep in mind.

1 The ideas below come from Alfred Kelly, "Writing a Good History Paper," Hamilton College History Department, 2008, http://www.hamilton.edu/documents/writing-center/WritingGoodHistoryPaper.pdf.

Avoid anachronistic thinking and writing. One of the most common problems that students have when writing about the past is that they apply present-day thinking to historical events, people, or issues. This can be as simple—but still as consequential—as misunderstanding what a historical figure was saying because a particular word or phrase that the figure used has changed in meaning since then. One scholar of historical thinking gives the example of a history instructor at a university in Northern Ireland who has his students analyze a 1562 quotation from Queen Elizabeth that refers to the inhabitants of Ireland as "mere Irish." The instructor's Irish students often take offense at this, only to discover, when they consult the *Oxford English Dictionary*, that in the sixteenth century "mere" meant "pure, unadulterated." Elizabeth, that is, wasn't denigrating the Irish by calling them "mere," as an anachronistic modern-day reading of her words would make us think; she simply meant that they were *completely* Irish.[2]

On a more complex level, anachronistic thinking can involve importing present-day concepts or categories that did not exist (at least not in the same way) in the past. For example, asking whether a given historical figure—particularly one who lived centuries ago—was gay, or arguing that they were, presupposes that people in the past thought about sexuality, sexual identity, and sexual orientation in the same way that we do today. In fact, many different understandings of sexuality have existed in different times and places throughout history. Although homosexual *acts* have been a part of human behavior for all of recorded history, the modern categories of homosexuality and heterosexuality only began to be formed, in the sense that we conceive of them today, in Europe and America in the late nineteenth century. In short, it is anachronistic to apply those categories to people who lived further back in time and would not have thought of themselves as gay—or, for that matter, straight—in a modern sense.

Lastly, viewing the past through the lens of the present can cause students to judge historical figures according to today's standards, instead of trying to understand those figures in the context of their own time. In the light of present-day attitudes—and with the benefit of hindsight—it can be easy, for example, to criticize Abraham Lincoln for not moving more quickly to commit the federal government to the abolition of slavery during the Civil War. Plenty of abolitionists, of course, did criticize Lincoln at the time on

2 Sam Wineburg, "Historical Thinking Is Unnatural—and Immensely Important: An Interview with Sam Wineburg," in *Recent Themes in Historical Thinking: Historians in Conversation*, ed. Donald A. Yerxa (University of South Carolina Press, 2008), 36.

exactly these grounds. But it would be anachronistic to give too much weight to these abolitionist critics (who comprised a small minority) simply because their values align with those of most of us today. In doing so, we would be writing off or ignoring the perspectives of the many other Civil War–era Americans with different ideas about race, slavery, and the war rather than trying to understand those different ideas in their own right.

To be sure, it is not entirely possible to divorce ourselves from current-day values, concepts, and perspectives when studying the past—nor is it entirely desirable. Without getting into the debates about presentism (see p. 35 regarding this term) that have recently roiled the academic historical community, we can say that if an overly value-laden approach to historical study is dangerous, so is a completely value-free approach.[3] To stick with the example just given, while we should avoid leveling too harsh of a judgment on Lincoln's policies and actions early in the Civil War based on present-day standards of racial justice, it would be equally misguided (if not more so) to jettison standards of racial justice altogether when studying the Civil War. For instance, it would be foolhardy to claim that we cannot or should not judge the actions of the Southern secessionists who took up arms against the federal government. They did so, after all, so that they could continue holding millions of African Americans in bondage. Or to give a different example, no one studying Nazi Germany's conduct in World War II can avoid reckoning with the role that Nazi racial ideology played in that conduct. An overtly "objective," non-judgmental interpretation of the atrocities that German forces committed during their invasion of the Soviet Union might ascribe those atrocities solely to Germany's desire to win the war quickly. But that interpretation would fail to take into account the critically important fact that German forces viewed the inhabitants of the Soviet Union as subhuman. It remains important, however, to try to set present-day perspectives and assumptions aside when analyzing historical events and actors, at least to start with, and attempt to understand these events and actors on their own terms. That requires a bit of imagination—namely, putting ourselves in the shoes of those we're studying, as best we can.

3 For accounts of this recent debate, which was sparked by criticisms of presentism made by James Sweet, the president of the American Historical Association, in an August 2022 column, see Colleen Flaherty, "Presentism, Race and Trolls," *Inside Higher Ed*, August 21, 2022, https://www.insidehighered.com/news/2022/08/22/white-nationalist-enters-historians-debate-presentism; and Emma Green, "The Right Side of History," *New Yorker*, March 7, 2023, https://www.newyorker.com/news/annals-of-education/the-right-side-of-history.

Remember your chronology. It's very frustrating to read a history paper that makes inexplicable jumps between time periods, or simply doesn't seem to reflect the student's clear understanding of what happened, and in what order. Simply put, "chronology is the backbone of history."[4] Make sure that you know the timeline of the events you're describing and that you keep dates in the front of your mind when writing and organizing your paper.

This isn't to say that you need to write as though you are listing events in a timeline (first, this happened, second, this happened, and so forth). Rather, what it does mean is that you have to have a pretty good sense of the sequence of events you're writing about so that you don't make assumptions that confuse your reader. Imagine, for example, how perplexing it would be to discuss the Civil Rights policies of Lyndon Johnson's presidential administration *before* moving back in time to discuss those of the earlier Kennedy administration, without making clear to your reader that you had a strong argumentative reason for addressing each administration's policies in this reverse chronological order.

You're over-quoting. As I have indicated in previous chapters, historians are very careful when selecting quotations that they want to insert into their writing. When quoting secondary sources, err on the side of "less is more." Most of the time, you should paraphrase or summarize (and add a citation, of course) so that your reader knows how you have integrated other authors' arguments into your own writing. When you over-quote—especially passages from secondary sources—it appears you are trying to fill space. It also suggests that you don't trust your own ability to write about your subject.

When it comes to primary sources, confine the quotation to the portion of the source that's most applicable to your argument. Make sure to analyze the quotation and explain how it applies to your argument.

This is a "one-draft wonder."[5] It's really hard, if not impossible, to write a good history paper at the last minute. Even the finest, most experienced writers need time to write a draft, let it sit for a few days, and return to it when their minds are fresh. One draft can turn into multiple drafts, as we reconsider new plans of organization or new ways of articulating our argument.

When you don't leave yourself enough time to revise, your paper is sure to contain numerous mistakes that will get in the way of your argument.

---

4 Kelley, "Writing a Good History Paper," 4.

5 Kelley, "Writing a Good History Paper," 10.

The finished product will pale in comparison to a paper that received the time it deserved. Devote time to revision of content as well as to mechanics and you'll avoid seeing this type of comment on a final submission.

Too many generalizations and vague statements. Historical writing places enormous emphasis on precision. If your paper makes statements such as "People say *X*," "Everyone does *Y*," or "American citizens want *Z*," your instructor will probably ask who you're talking about! If you use a sentence such as "The 1960s was a decade of change," you'll get asked, "What kind of change?" or "What happened?" You get the idea.

I find it helpful to tell students that their job is to set the scene so that readers can feel like they are standing in the middle of the story. If half of your facts are missing, you won't really have done your job. Too many vague statements make it look like you have run out of things to say and are trying to reach a minimum length requirement. If you find yourself making generalizations and cannot figure out how to clarify what you've written, you need to hit the sources again and do some more thinking.

You are using inappropriate sources. Historical writing at the college level requires reliance on scholarly books and journal articles, not popular magazines, encyclopedia articles, and blog posts (see pp. 70–71). I have often found that though they have discovered appropriate sources, students are reluctant to dig into them. This takes time, of course, and you need to crack the books before the night before the paper is due. But there's a reason why that time is well-spent. It will demonstrate that you have a grasp of what experts have said about your topic and how your thesis fits into the larger scholarly conversation on it.

A red flag to any instructor is if the same source pops up in the footnotes over and over again. Over-reliance on one source is a bad sign for any research paper. Why should I believe a source if it hasn't been corroborated? Sometimes students will think that if they have a long bibliography, the instructor won't notice that only one source features prominently in their argument. Footnotes make it very easy to tell which sources you've relied upon.

You are accepting your evidence without criticism. In Chapter 6, we discussed the questions you need to ask of primary and secondary sources. When we ask these questions, it's because we want to make sure we keep them in mind when writing the paper itself. If you present just one side of a story as legitimate, without any reference to corroborating data or alternative perspectives, your reader will start to question the credibility of your argument.

Let's be clear: You can have significant criticisms of a source and still use it to support your argument. I don't mean to imply that you should criticize a source to the point that it's not viable. But you do need to remember that every source has flaws and that no one source can stand on its own.

This paper is descriptive, not analytical. One of the main differences between high school and college-level writing that we discussed at the very beginning of this book was the need to move beyond mere summary of the facts to an interpretation of historical evidence. Though students I have taught seemed to understand this in theory, they often had a tough time when they started writing. It may be helpful to think of it this way. When you summarize, you explain what happened, who was involved, and when and where an incident took place. When you analyze, you dig into questions of why and how the event happened, and of whether, how, and to what extent the event might have affected or influenced others.

Students who rely too heavily on encyclopedias, or on one or two secondary sources to the exclusion of all others, are most prone to writing papers that are overly descriptive and insufficiently analytical. Similarly, writers who don't adequately engage with their primary sources are bound to have this problem. Think about it: the collection of primary sources you've amassed is what distinguishes your paper from others on the same topic. Your primary sources enable you to support your explanation or argument. If you ignore them, you can't sustain an argument at all. All you can do is repeat what others have already said.

You don't have a clear thesis throughout. Perhaps the most common problem students have when they write history papers has to do with the thesis statement. Students often begin writing without truly understanding their argument. They might start out with a great idea of what it could be, but then lose steam a couple pages later. The last page or two of the paper veers off course as a result. Alternatively, the thesis might be poorly written, making it difficult to use as a roadmap for the paper's organization.

Think of your thesis as the foundation on which the rest of the paper is built: if it's shaky, the whole paper falls apart. In a history paper, a thesis should be stated for the first time within the introduction, and then systematically demonstrated and developed throughout the paper. Or, to put it another way, "Your reader should always know where your argument has come from, where it is now, and where it is going."[6]

6 Kelley, "Writing a Good History Paper," 2.

Taking the time to construct and revise a thesis will go a long way to ensuring the success of your research paper. You may actually enjoy the writing process, or at least find it less frustrating, because every paragraph won't seem like a new challenge. With a good thesis in mind, you simply know what's coming, and what you have to do next to make your paper work.

Style Conventions

In addition to following broader content conventions, history papers also typically adhere to a particular writing style. Some of the foremost conventions of this writing style are as follows:

Avoid passive voice. To use the active voice, start with the historical actor or actors you're talking about (the subject of the sentence) and explain what they did. Students frequently get stuck in the passive voice by putting the object of the action first. For instance, "The election was won by the Democratic Party" instead of "The Democratic Party won the election." Passive voice inserts unnecessary "to be" verbs into your sentences, which makes the essay read quite clumsily. More importantly, using the passive voice implicitly diminishes the agency of the historical actors you are writing about. If, for example, you write "The 1955 Montgomery bus boycott was led by Martin Luther King, Jr." rather than "Martin Luther King, Jr. led the 1955 Montgomery bus boycott," you grammatically sideline King in a way that makes his actions seem less significant. The goal of historical scholarship is to provide a better, clearer, more precise understanding of what people in the past did, how and why they did it, and what the effects of their actions were. Using the passive voice interferes with this goal by literally positioning the people who did things in the past as afterthoughts in your sentences. As much as possible, you should therefore write in the active voice.[7]

I will never forget that when I handed in one of my first papers as a first-year college student, my English professor put a circle around all my "to be" verbs and connected them with lines. I was really angry and annoyed at the time, but it made the point pretty well. It certainly taught me about the problems associated with passive voice.

Use the past tense consistently when discussing the past. Remember that whenever you write about historical events, you should write in the

7 On active vs. passive voice, see Kelley, "Writing a Good History Paper," 11–12.

past tense. If you are describing what a historian says about the past, however—when drawing on a secondary source—you should use the present tense. So, "Historian X *argues* [present] that Kennedy *was* [past] a good president."[8]

Be concise and avoid repetitive language. Historians try to eliminate unnecessary verbiage. If it takes you three sentences to say what you could more efficiently say in one, that's a sign that you should cut out some of the excess.

Note that it's always easier to edit someone else's writing than your own, so don't expect to be able to eliminate redundant language in your draft at the last minute. The best strategy (as usual) is to start early, write a draft of your paper, and let it sit for a few days untouched. When you return to it, you'll find more places to cut than you ever thought possible.[9]

Avoid unclear or confusing language. This may seem obvious, but you need to write in a way that's understandable not only to you, but to someone who knows next to nothing about your topic. Unlike many other disciplines, History tends to use very little jargon. If you give your essay to an intelligent person who doesn't know much about your topic, they should be able to understand your writing. The advantage is that you should be able to give your draft to friends or family members and have them identify language that lacks clarity.

If you do need to explain a theory or any type of advanced concept, make sure you understand what you're saying and are describing it clearly. I found that students often employed a synonym, for instance, without understanding that the word they're using did not quite fit their intended context.[10]

Write paragraphs that aren't overly long and contain clear topic sentences. Occasionally, I found that a student's five-page paper contained just two paragraphs. This is not a good sign because it implies a clear lack of organization and logical progression of ideas. Visually, it is completely overwhelming to read a paragraph that seems to go on forever. Paragraph breaks are natural breathing points for readers—in particular, for instructors who are following your writing very closely and trying to keep track of your logic.[11]

---

8 Kelley, "Writing a Good History Paper," 13. Kelley provides other examples that are helpful as well.

9 Kelley, "Writing a Good History Paper," 11.

10 Kelley, "Writing a Good History Paper," 4, 12.

11 Kelley, "Writing a Good History Paper," 12–13.

I frequently broke up paragraphs myself when reading overly long passages in a student's essay. I did this because I couldn't remember what students were saying otherwise. The reason that we put one major idea in each paragraph is because that is how our brains work: we can only digest so much at once.

Include transition sentences that make sense. Students frequently forget that the job of the writer is to be a tour guide—to provide calm and steady leadership while escorting their reader through unfamiliar territory. It's hard, not to mention frustrating, to follow an essay when logical transitions between paragraphs are lacking. Poor or non-existent transition sentences will quickly cause your reader to lose track of what you're talking about, undermining your thesis.

One common example of a poor transition is a paragraph that starts with "Another idea" or "Another example." The word "another" does not describe a relationship to a thesis; it simply adds something else to the mix.[12]

Integrate quotations so that they make sense. Quotations should be incorporated into your writing so that they make sense grammatically. I explain this in depth in Chapter 14.

Avoid hyperbolic language. Since historical writing is typically very precise, the discipline frowns on exaggeration and hyperbole. If you say that a situation was a "disaster" or a "catastrophe," make sure the term fits. Resist the temptation to say that the president you're studying was "the worst" or "the best," as this language is entirely subjective, not to mention virtually meaningless in terms of argument.

See Online Companion Exercise 11
sites.broadviewpress.com/puzzle/chapter-11

Rules for Writing Papers in the Humanities

History shares a number of writing conventions with other humanities disciplines, especially regarding formality. Academic writing is formal writing.

12 Kelley, "Writing a Good History Paper," 16.

Formal doesn't mean "stuffy," though; it just means that proper grammar and syntax are essential. Here are some other basic rules to keep in mind.[13]

Avoid clichés and slang. A cliché is a phrase that is used commonly in speech to express a sentiment, but tends to cheapen formal writing. Some examples:

- Martin Luther King, Jr.'s speech was really *over the top*.
- We thought that candidate's proposal was a *breath of fresh air*.
- She wasn't working hard; she was really *out to lunch*.
- That politician *phoned it in*.
- She figured she had that job offer *in the bag*.

Beyond their informality, the bigger problem with clichés is that—as the famous British writer George Orwell pointed out in 1946—they substitute for original thought. Resorting to clichés—in Orwell's words, "throwing your mind open and letting the ready-made phrases come crowding in"[14]—is a way of avoiding having to think deeply and clearly about what you want to say and coming up with an original, distinctive way to say it. Clichés, as Orwell puts it, "will construct your sentences for you—even think your thoughts for you."[15] Just like the passive voice (which Orwell also recommends avoiding), using clichés diminishes agency—in this case, your own agency as a writer.

As with clichés, avoid slang in academic writing. Not sure if something you say frequently is considered slang? If it turns up online in an urban dictionary, chances are that it is. Similarly, avoid the type of shorthand language that you'd use in a text message. Beyond being overly conversational, slang words are often unfamiliar to those of us who are more advanced in years (read: older) than you. Slang can also be obscure and alienating to readers who do not belong to the particular subculture in which it originated.

Contractions. It's best to avoid contractions (such as the one at the beginning of this sentence) in formal academic writing. Beyond their informality, certain contractions can also be confusing for your readers—and

---

13 The suggestions in this section on humanities conventions come from Richard A. Nanian, "Some Stylistic Conventions for Writing in the Humanities," George Mason University, Spring 2020, http://mason.gmu.edu/~rnanian/201conventions.html.

14 George Orwell, "Politics and the English Language," in *A Collection of Essays* (Harcourt, 1981), 165.

15 Orwell, "Politics and the English Language," 165.

potentially also for you as a writer. At some point in your writing life, it's likely that you've puzzled over "you're" versus "your," "they're" versus "their" versus "there," and—probably the worst of all!—"it's" versus "its." In all these cases, your potential confusion as a writer over which is correct, and the confusion that getting it incorrect would cause your reader, can be avoided by eschewing the contraction. Instead of using the contraction "it's," just get in the habit of always writing "it is." That way, you'll never run the risk of confusing this contraction with the possessive pronoun "its."

(In case you weren't already aware of it, the preceding paragraph should have made clear that this rule against using contractions is one of several rules of formal academic writing that I'm not following in this book for the simple reason that it is not a work of formal historical scholarship. In other words, you can see here a good example of different writing conventions at work: Where academic writing emphasizes formality, handbooks such as this one emphasize accessibility, and the conventions governing their writing therefore permit a certain amount—but only a certain amount—of informality. So if it seems like the message here is "do as I say, not as I do," it's not actually that arbitrary. What you'll be doing in your history paper is a different kind of writing, with different accompanying conventions, than what I'm doing here.)

Use of the first person. It used to be considered bad form to ever use the first person in academic writing because scholars feared they'd appear less objective if they did so. More recently, however, the rule has become a bit less stringent. The occasional use of the word "I" is not necessarily a terrible thing, provided the habit isn't abused. In my opinion, it's still a good idea to avoid the first person as much as possible in a scholarly essay. Ask your instructor about their personal preference.

Should you wish to use the first person, here are some guidelines. "I know" comes across as a bit over-confident, if not arrogant; "I believe" implies a lack of evidence to support your assertion; "I think" indicates that you don't have much confidence in what you're saying. Avoid "I feel," as it suggests a psychological or emotional state of mind rather than a stance based on facts and evidence. And, please, don't refer to yourself in the third person.[16] ("Valerie Thaler thinks x.") That's really awkward and quite stilted. If you do, then your instructor might write what I almost wrote in the margin of some papers next to these phrases: "Do you agree?"

16 Nanian, "Some Stylistic Conventions for Writing in the Humanities."

Avoid Latin abbreviations such as etc. or e.g. Though it was once considered acceptable, it's best to list a couple of examples rather than use these abbreviations in academic writing.

Using names. When you mention a person's name for the first time, use the full name (first and last). In subsequent cases, simply refer to the individual by the last name. If you happen to refer to one of the scholars that you cite, do the same thing (although you could just refer to historians in the footnotes).

Whatever you do, don't change course midstream and start using the first and last name again, or the first name in isolation. I had students refer to historical figures by their first names in both exams and papers, and I found myself commenting, "This is not your friend." Again, it's just too casual a tone for academic writing.

Numbers. A good rule of thumb is that whole numbers that can be written in one or two words should be spelled out. So, you'd write out seven, eight hundred, or twenty-three. If the number is three words long, you can write it out *or* use the number itself: 400,000 or four hundred thousand. Choose one option for three-word numbers and stick to it consistently. If you wish to use a number that contains a decimal, or is four or more words long, always write just the number. The only exception is dates, which should always be written as numerals, not as words.

Complimentary language. Avoid empty praise of historical figures that contributes nothing of substance to your argument. I can't tell you how many times I've read papers that start with "The Beatles were one of the greatest bands of all time," or "Martin Luther King, Jr. was a terrific Civil Rights leader." While not untrue, these statements don't belong in academic writing.

Referring to titles within your essay. Book titles should be in italics, while poems, articles, or essays in a collection or anthology should be in quotation marks.[17]

17 Nanian, "Some Stylistic Conventions for Writing in the Humanities."

CHAPTER 12

The Elements of a Historical Research Paper

What's your end goal for this project? What do you hope to say you've been able to accomplish? Every student responds to this question differently, of course. Some students might answer "When I get to ten pages, I'll be happy" (or whatever the page minimum). Others might say, "I will have been successful if I get an A." Some might be okay with a B. If you're reading this book carefully, I doubt you'd be satisfied with much less than a B. In this chapter, I'm going to share my perspective, as an instructor, on what makes a historical research paper successful—or unsuccessful.

The Reader's Perspective

I put this criterion first, because students frequently forget how important it is. A history paper works well when I can understand what the student is saying, and when the argument progresses logically and clearly. I loved reading these papers (and I don't say that casually). When reading them, I would think, "Now that's why I became a historian."

Your job, as a writer of a research paper, is to take your readers on a journey that has a beginning, a middle, and an end. It's to figure out the clearest and most logical path of getting from point A to point B, and provide the necessary leadership and guidance along the way. If you succeed in conducting this journey, your readers will feel very comfortable following you, and won't need to stop to ask questions every other minute about where you're planning to go.

The ticket to crafting a smooth journey for your readers is remembering their perspective at all times. You should assume that your readers are quite unfamiliar with your topic. They are surely intelligent and have a basic knowledge of history. But they do not have the expertise on your topic that you should have at this point in your investigation. Your obligation as the writer is to provide the necessary historical context for your readers to understand your research problem, and then to take them through the process by which you are introducing, developing, and defending your thesis statement.

The best writers test out their prose on others to make sure they're on the right track. Since historical writing should be relatively jargon-free, you should be able to give your introductory paragraph to (for instance) a friend or a family member and say, "Tell me what you think I'm trying to say, and tell me what doesn't make sense to you." When you have written a draft, your reader should be able to indicate if there are points in the paper where your argument falls apart, where you've departed from your central idea, or where a primary source seems inadequately discussed.

You may be thinking, "This all sounds great. But my friends and family have their own work to do. How will they have time to read my writing?" This is a fair point; sometimes, if others do not have the time or ability to look over your work, you will have to be your own reader. But the only way you can do this well is if you leave ample time for the draft you have written to sit for a few days, so that you almost don't remember what you wrote and how you wrote it. Then when you return to it, you'll have a fresh perspective and will be able to revise effectively. Otherwise, as the writer, you're too close to your own writing to make substantive changes.

I could almost always tell when students had not provided themselves that extra time. If I met with a student after the paper had been graded, and tried to explain where they went wrong, they'd read a paragraph and admit, "That's not what I meant to say." At that point, they were doing what they should have done before the paper was due: take a look at it from a fresh perspective.

If a writer does not keep their reader in mind, the reader will struggle to get through the paper. Instead of being able to appreciate what the writer has to say, the reader will spend most of their time trying to figure out what the writer is *trying* to say. The reader will be thrilled to get to the end, but not because they're satisfied with a job well done and convinced by the writer's argument: they're relieved to be done. If the writer *does* keep the reader's perspective in mind, the experience of reading the paper is extremely rewarding.

More so than any other, the significance of this element extends far beyond the history paper and into every other academic discipline or professional endeavor on which you might embark. Whether you write an English paper, deliver a scientific presentation, narrate a podcast, or even just revise a résumé for submission, you need to make sure you're remembering your audience's perspective. This means stepping outside of your own head and considering what matters most to those consuming the information you present.

The Title

Take a few minutes and think of a title that is better than what I've seen hundreds of times: "History Paper." Or, even more creative: "History 101 Paper." The title also shouldn't just state the name of the person you examined ("Benjamin Franklin"). Remember, you're in college! You don't want your paper to look like a fourth-grade book report. This doesn't mean the title needs to be twenty words long, but it should at least make reference to your main argument. (Also, please spell your professor's name right on the first page—not doing so isn't a very good move.)

The Introduction

The actor Will Rogers said, "You never get a second chance to make a first impression." It's a statement that some (older) people associate with Head & Shoulders shampoo commercials from the 1980s. But it's also the purpose of the introduction to your research paper. Botching it will do your paper a lot of harm. The first two paragraphs (give or take) set the tone for the rest of your paper, telling your reader whether you know what you're talking about. I'd recommend revising the introduction up until the time you have finished the paper, to make sure you do what you say you're going to do in the course of your paper.

An introduction requires a number of elements: 1) a short explanation of relevant historical context, including a definition of any key terms you'll be using; 2) a statement of the research problem (or question); 3) brief reference to what types of primary sources you have investigated; and 4) a carefully formulated thesis statement.

Establish the historical context. You should assume that your reader is someone in your undergraduate classroom and has a general knowledge of history but does not have extensive background on your topic. It's important to determine what the reader actually needs to know to understand your research problem and thesis. Set the scene quickly for your reader so that it is clear what you are talking about (the who, what, when, where, and why). If you are going to be referring to one portion of a larger topic, specify what will concern you. For instance, I wouldn't just say that I'm studying the Civil Rights Movement: I'd discuss the relevant place, event, actors, dates, etc. If there are any terms that could be misconstrued if not defined, now is the time to define them clearly.

Students often ask how much background they need to provide. It is really difficult to provide a general answer to this question, as it is a matter of personal judgment and will of course depend on your choice of topic. However, this is the type of question that friends or family members may be able to answer. Have them read the introduction and paraphrase your main points. If a major piece of the puzzle is missing, you'll know pretty quickly that you need to provide more context.

State your research problem. What is your research question or problem? After you have introduced the relevant historical context, go ahead and explain the precise issue that you found intriguing—the problem that you sought to solve over the course of your research. Your language should be clear, concise, and engaging. Remember, this is the issue that has framed your research and kept you invested in this project for the last few weeks (or months), and your job is to explain why your reader should care about it.

Students often asked me if they needed to write out their question in the introduction, as they found this to be stylistically awkward. You don't need to write out the precise question, per se. But you do need to give the reader a very clear sense of what issue drove your research.

Refer to the types of sources that you'll consult, or your strategy for answering this question. What types of primary sources led you to your thesis? What's your game plan for using them? Listing each source is not necessary. But if you've found government documents and speeches to be extremely useful in shedding light on your research topic, you can say that here. If your sources can be divided into public and private categories, mention that also. Just provide some indication of how you're going to go about answering your question so your reader knows you have a clear agenda in mind.[1]

Spell out your thesis. The thesis statement should be the last sentence (or so) of your introduction, and should indicate your central argument for the body of the paper. If your thesis has been well-formulated and carefully constructed, it will make sense when placed at the end of the introductory paragraph. If you edit your thesis in the course of writing your paper, which you almost surely will, you will need to make adjustments to your introductory paragraph in accordance with the revised thesis statement.

Lastly, stay away from the "beginning of time" introduction. A lot of students make the mistake of trying to sound overly lofty in their introduction. You have not done enough research to speak about how your topic compares to "all periods of history" or to events "since the beginning of time." It sounds pretty silly when I say it this way, but you'd be surprised how frequently such phrases turned up in students' introductory paragraphs.[2]

See Online Companion Exercise 12A
sites.broadviewpress.com/puzzle/chapter-12

The Body Paragraphs

Let's assume that you now have a solid working introduction. Here's what to aim for in the bulk of the paper.

The paragraphs connect logically to the thesis. Your argument develops in a fashion that matches the thesis, so the reader does not have to deal with unexpected twists and turns. You don't have to spell out every detail of the paper in the introduction, but your thesis should provide enough of a framework that the rest of your paper follows a trajectory that makes sense. If you find yourself unable to figure out what comes next, chances are your thesis needs to be revised.

1 Patrick Rael, "The Three Parts of a History Paper," *Reading, Writing, and Researching for History: A Guide for College Students* (Bowdoin College, 2004), https://courses.bowdoin.edu/writing-guides/.

2 Rael's guide provides very concise and helpful guidance for students, including mention of this common mistake.

Paragraphs connect logically to one another. You should be able to read just the first sentences of each paragraph and see a logical progression. If you are starting a paragraph with "Another reason" or "Another aspect," that's a sign that you have more work to do.

The paragraphs each contain clearly focused topic sentences. It's imperative that each paragraph deal with one idea at a time and doesn't get too convoluted. I strongly recommend that you keep your paragraph lengths to a minimum of four sentences and a maximum of one double-spaced page. Students think that excessively long paragraphs are not a problem—but they are. This is especially the case in a short paper. Oversized paragraphs usually veer off topic and are conceptually overwhelming to the reader, who cannot keep so many ideas straight at once.

The writer supports the argument with evidence from a variety of primary and secondary sources. Your argument falls apart if it doesn't have the foundation provided by sources. Equally critical is that you don't let quotations or paraphrases stand on their own, but instead you actually explain how they contribute to the point you are trying to make.

The writer considers counterarguments or different points of view. While the chief purpose of your research paper is to argue a particular point, don't forget to consider perspectives different from your own. You might find scholars who have interpreted your subject differently than you have, or alternative readings of primary sources that could lead you to a different conclusion. When a writer addresses these appropriately—even in just a sentence or two when it makes sense—I know that she has thought carefully about the topic. (See Chapter 9.)

The writer includes citations (footnotes) every time a source is paraphrased, summarized, or quoted. Papers should cite sources frequently, and these citations should be done properly. If I see a citation only attached to quotations, I begin to worry that a student has plagiarized, either intentionally or unintentionally. (See Chapter 13.)

The writer uses quotations sparingly. The chosen quotations contribute significantly to the argument. Papers that quote indiscriminately suggest that a writer is unsure of themselves and is employing quotations just to fill space. (See Chapter 14.)

The paper is consistently strong in its argument and writing from beginning to end. Again, it all goes back to giving yourself time to write and revise your writing. It's often the case that a paper starts off very strong with a concise introduction and a persuasive thesis. But a couple pages later, the writer seems to run out of steam.

It's also worth pointing out once again the importance of not multi-tasking when you are writing or revising a history paper. Why? Because if you write one paragraph, text your friends, check social media, then write another paragraph, your paper is going to sound really choppy. It'll lose the flow and continuity that come from sustained focus on a single task.

The Conclusion

Your conclusion gives your reader their last impression of your argument, as well as of you as a writer. You want to take the opportunity to restate your main argument. Do not use the exact same words that you used in your introduction. Try to paraphrase. You also want to tell your reader why it matters that you did this research in the first place. In other words, you want to answer the "So what?" question. Why should I care about this topic? Does your research raise an issue that needs to be investigated further? How does it connect to current scholarship? Writing a conclusion is a bit tricky, because you don't want to start a new paper by bringing up too much unfamiliar information, but you *do* want to keep your reader interested and wanting to learn more about your topic. It's a delicate balance.[3]

The Bibliography

Students often fail to spend much time on their bibliographies, listing sources out of alphabetical order or not paying attention to proper formatting. This is tedious work—but it's actually pretty easy if you give yourself enough time. A poorly formatted or incomplete bibliography suggests carelessness on the part of the student: you can avoid this. (See Chapter 13 for guidance.)

Proofreading

Overall, the paper is clean and has been proofread. It is written well and does not contain typographical or spelling errors. A poorly edited essay will

3 Rael, "The Three Parts of a History Paper."

reflect poorly on you, even if your argument is sophisticated. Submitting a historical essay rife with mechanical errors is a bit like handing in a résumé full of typos. Your reader will have a hard time overlooking the problems because these tell the reader, "This paper didn't matter enough for me to clean up the errors." Some proofreading suggestions:

- *Read your essay aloud.* You will catch many more mistakes than if you just read it silently.
- *Print out your essay and read it in hard copy.* Even though you'll probably be submitting your essay online, it's worth taking the time to print it out so you can detect mistakes you would likely have missed otherwise.
- *Never trust spellcheck to correct all of your mistakes.* It will not catch everything. It gets especially confused by homonyms.
- *Allow plenty of time.* The best proofreading doesn't take place an hour before the paper is due—regardless of what your friends might tell you.
- *Read your topic sentences in reverse order.* This is another strategy for catching mistakes in logic.
- *Read the essay sentence by sentence, but starting from the end.* You will catch sentence-level errors that way.[4]
- *Visit your college's writing lab to sit down with a tutor.* Many universities have dramatically expanded their writing programs, providing tutors for every stage of the writing process. You would be foolish not to take advantage of these amazing resources.
- *Check out the frequently confused words below, and make sure you didn't make any major errors.*

4 These suggestions for proofreading come from "Proofreading: Where Do I Begin?," Purdue Online Writing Lab, accessed March 29, 2025, https://owl.purdue.edu/owl/general_writing/the_writing_process/proofreading/index.html.

Fifty Frequently Confused Words

accept/except	To *accept* is to receive or agree to something. *Except* is an adjective referring to one left out.
adverse/averse	*Adverse* is an adjective meaning unfavorable. *Averse* is an adjective referring to one's opposition to something. The medicine had *adverse* side effects. She was *averse* to the decision her colleagues had made.
affect/effect	*Affect* is usually a verb and *effect* is usually a noun, as in: How did that *affect* me? It had the desired *effect*. But: *Affect* can be a noun, if referring to facial expression. *Effect* is a verb when used in the context of bringing about change.
aisle/isle	An *aisle* refers to the empty space between rows. An *isle* refers to an island.
allowed/aloud	*Allowed* means permitted. *Aloud* is audible or capable of being heard.
allude/elude	To *allude* is to make reference to something. To *elude* is to avoid or evade.
allusion/ illusion	An *allusion* is a reference to something within a text. An *illusion* is an inaccurate impression.
altar/alter	An *altar* is a sacred space in a church. To *alter* is to change something.
altogether/ all together	*Altogether* is usually an adverb meaning completely. *All together* describes events happening at once. She was *altogether* certain that she'd receive a good grade. The conductor asked the musicians to play the piece *all together*.
alumnus/ alumna/ alumni/ alumnae	An *alumnus* is a male graduate of an institution. An *alumna* is a female graduate. *Alumni* are graduates (male, or male and female). *Alumnae* are graduates (female only).
assent/ascent	*Assent* refers to agreement. *Ascent* means movement upward.
autobiography/ biography	An *autobiography* is a book someone writes about themself. A *biography* is a study of a person's life written by a scholar.
based on	Don't say, "I based my ideas *off of* ..."; do say, "I based my ideas *on* ..."

beside/besides	*Beside* is a preposition meaning next to or near. *Besides* refers to except for, or in addition to.
bias/biased	Bias is a noun; biased is an adjective that means that one casts judgment according to previously held assumptions. You can *have a bias* but you *are biased*.
book/novel	A *novel* is a work of fiction. A historical text is a *book*, but not a novel.
capital/Capitol	A *capital* is a city that serves as the seat of government; it is also another word for wealth. The *Capitol* is the building for members of the US Congress.
centers on	Don't say, "This idea *centers around* the theory ..." Do say, "This idea *centers on* the theory ..."
cite/site/sight	You *cite* a source, or include *citations* in your paper. What a *sight* my eyes have witnessed! I have visited that *site* on the internet.
climactic/ climatic	*Climactic* is an adjective referring to the climax of a story. *Climatic* is an adjective referring to climate or weather conditions.
compliment/ complement	A *compliment* is a flattering remark about someone. A *complement* is something that completes something else.
conscious/ conscience	Don't say, "When I woke up in the morning, I was *conscience*." Do say, "When I woke up in the morning, I was *conscious*. But my *conscience* bothered me because I slept through my alarm."
council/ counsel	A *council* is a governing body or committee. *Counsel* is a noun meaning advice, often used in a legal context. The verb *counsel* means to provide advice, as would a counselor.
decent/ descent/ dissent	*Decent* is an adjective referring to basic goodness. *Descent* refers to movement downward. *Dissent* means disagreement.
discreet/ discrete	*Discreet* refers to modest, unobtrusive behavior. *Discrete* refers to separate or distinct parts.
disinterested/ uninterested	*Disinterest* refers to a state of emotional distance. *Uninterest* refers to a lack of interest in something, or boredom. She found the movie *uninteresting;* she even fell asleep. The voters evinced *disinterest* due to a particularly difficult election season. They just wanted it to end.
elicit/illicit	*Elicit* means to obtain information from, such as in legal matters. *Illicit* refers to an illegal act.

emigrate from vs. immigrate to	*Emigrate* refers to the act of leaving a country. *Immigrate* refers to the act of entering a country.
eminent/ imminent	*Eminent* refers to prominence or stature in leadership (a religious figure may be referred to as "His Eminence"). *Imminent* refers to an event that is about to happen.
everyday/ every day	*Everyday* is an adjective for something occurring frequently or routinely. *Every day* is used to refer to the progression of days.
farther/further	Use *farther* when comparing distances only. Use *further* when comparing degrees/extents or times. She ran *farther* than he did in the marathon. Can you read *further* for next week?
healthful/ healthy	*Healthful* refers to a good habit. *Healthy* describes a fit person.
historic/ historical	*Historical* describes anything associated with history. *Historic* refers to something particularly noteworthy.
it's/its	*It's* is the conjunction it is. *Its* refers to the possessive.
lead vs. led	*Lead* is the present tense of providing direction (to lead a group); *lead* is also a chemical element. *Led* is the past tense of lead.
less vs. fewer	Use *less* when you are talking about a singular noun, and *fewer* when dealing with a plural noun, such as: She had *fewer* chocolate chips than he had. I weighed *less* than my sister.
loose/lose	*Loose* is an adjective that refers to the opposite of tight. *Lose* is a verb meaning the opposite of win.
much/many	Use *much* when referring to a singular noun, and *many* when dealing with a plural noun. I bought *much* water with *many* dollars.
principal/ principle	As a noun, *principal* is the person in charge of a school. As an adjective, *principal* refers to something of importance. The noun *principle* refers to an article of faith. The school *principal* spoke of the *principal* objectives for the school year, all of which centered on core *principles*.
regardless	*Regardless* is a word meaning no matter what, but *irregardless* is not a standard word and should therefore not be used in formal writing.

rein/reign	*Rein* is a verb that means retaining control; it can also refer to straps to control a horse. *Reign* is the political term for one leader. The queen's *reign* lasted five years; she had to *rein* in the troops. The cowboy held the *reins* on the horse.
statue/statute	A *statue* is a piece of sculpture. A *statute* is a law.
tenet/tenant	A *tenet* is a principle or idea. A *tenant* is a person who rents an apartment or house.
than/then	*Than* is used in comparative statements. She performed better *than* he did on the test. *Then* is a word related to time.
they're/their/ there	*They're* is the contraction of they are; *their* is the possessive; *there* refers to a place.
to/too/two	*To* is a preposition or refers to direction; *too* implies also; *two* refers to the number 2.
unique	*Unique* cannot be modified with any word (so, very, etc.) as it already means one of a kind.
who/that	Use *who* when referring to people; use *that* for things. The man *who* took the survey was quite thorough. The survey *that* we took was quite thorough.
who/whom	*Who* refers to the subject of a sentence; *whom* refers to the person who is the object of a preposition. She is the person *who* taught her. From *whom* did you learn that subject?
you're/your	*You're* is a contraction for you are. *Your* is possessive. Take *your* bag out. *You're* kidding me![5]

See Online Companion Exercises 12B and 12C
sites.broadviewpress.com/puzzle/chapter-12

5 This list is hardly exhaustive, of course. For more examples of commonly confused words, see "A List of Most Commonly Confused Words," *Merriam-Webster*, accessed March 29, 2025, https://www.merriam-webster.com/grammar/commonly-confused-words-list, or one of the many other examples easily found online.

CHAPTER 13

Chicago Style Made Logical

Understandably, students get frustrated when they discover that each discipline uses a particular citation style. They often asked me why they need to learn a different style for each paper they write and may even feel college instructors are just trying to make life tough for them. That's not the case. While there is no shortage of guidance online for writing notes and bibliography entries in the appropriate format (and I've included a partial list of format models toward the conclusion of this chapter), I think it's also helpful to answer the question of *why* Chicago Manual of Style (CMS) works well for historians. Is there a method to this madness? What is the internal logic of this system that makes it fit history's disciplinary conventions? I've found that when students understand the answers to these types of questions, they realize that citation is not merely a tedious exercise that adds further stress to paper writing. It actually has a purpose and functions in a particular way that fulfills the needs of the discipline in question. The goal of this chapter is to explain why historians use CMS and why that format makes the most sense for historical writing. By the end of the chapter, CMS won't seem like a random set of rules that you have to learn, but something that actually helps make citations easier to follow.[1]

1 See "CMOS Style Workshop," Chicago Style, Purdue Online Writing Lab, accessed March 29, 2025, https://owl.purdue.edu/owl/research_and_citation/chicago_manual_17th_edition/. Note that this article, and most of the references in this chapter, refer to the 17th edition of CMS, which was released in 2017. The 18th edition was released in 2024. The citation examples and guidance provided here have been updated to be consistent with [*continued*]

Let's first note an important source of confusion. When you search "Chicago Manual of Style," you'll see two documentation styles. One is called Notes and Bibliography (NB) and the other is Author-Date. The NB format is the one you want, as it's most commonly used in history papers. The Author-Date system is used in the sciences. I have had students get mixed up and use the Author-Date system by mistake, so I want to make this clear from the outset.

When to Cite Sources

Students sometimes come to college with misinformation about when they need to cite sources. Let's be completely clear from the start: You're always better off citing sources than not citing sources, especially if you're not sure if you have to. (See Chapter 15 for an explanation of "common knowledge.") Here's a brief review of the three cases in which sources need to be cited:

1. *When a source is quoted directly.* The vast majority of students realize that a direct quotation must always be cited in a note. (Make sure you've recorded the quotation accurately.)
2. *When a source is paraphrased.* If you have taken notes on a source and would like to restate the author's contributions in your own words, you need to cite the source just as you would a direct quotation.
3. *When a source is summarized.* Even if you write a one-sentence summary of an author's main argument, you need to cite the source.

CMS vs. MLA and APA

Historians use a combination of notes and bibliography, as opposed to styles that favor parenthetical citation, such as MLA (Modern Language Association) or APA (American Psychological Association). The term "notes" is shorthand for *footnotes* or *endnotes*. Notes are designated in a paper by small numerals throughout the text of the paper that appear slightly above

---

the 18th edition. For a list of citation updates in the 18th edition, see "What's New in the 18th Edition," Chicago Manual of Style Online, accessed March 30, 2025, https://www.chicagomanualofstyle.org/help-tools/what-s-new.html.

the line of text; they are in *superscript.* The corresponding note—where the citation is written—appears either at the bottom of the page (footnotes) or at the end of the paper before the bibliography (endnotes). The only difference between endnotes and footnotes is *where* they appear in the paper; other than that, they contain identical information and formatting. Your instructor will tell you which type of note they prefer. Both are easily created in Microsoft Word, and there are plenty of instructional videos on YouTube that help you learn how.

You're probably most familiar with MLA, which is the style you likely used for English papers in high school, and perhaps in other disciplines as well. MLA requires parenthetical citation in the text of the paper. Immediately after a quoted passage, for instance, you'd see a notation that includes the author of the text and the relevant page. The purpose of citations in English papers is chiefly to help your reader easily refer back to the original text you're discussing. Footnotes and endnotes are not too common in English papers because they are thought to distract from the flow of the paper itself. But when they do occur, they serve two specific purposes. First, they provide suggestions for additional reading (these are bibliographic notes). Second, content notes may sometimes be utilized in order to explain a point further.[2]

For papers written in the field of psychology or other behavioral sciences, APA style is required. APA formatting also uses parenthetical citation, but includes the author and the year the article was published. In APA-style papers, authors use references to refer to studies relevant to their own research. Footnotes or endnotes are rarely used in APA papers, except when an explanatory note is needed or to provide information related to copyright or permissions.[3]

Why Historians Use Footnotes

Historians use footnotes for purposes other than basic citation. Here's why historians use notes.

Historians use notes so that readers know exactly where they are getting information mentioned in the paper. The sheer variety of sources historians

2 "MLA Endnotes and Footnotes," MLA Style, Purdue Online Writing Lab, accessed November 22, 2024, https://owl.purdue.edu/owl/research_and_citation/mla_style.

3 "Footnotes and Endnotes," APA Style (7th Edition), Purdue Online Writing Lab, accessed November 22, 2024, https://owl.purdue.edu/owl/research_and_citation/apa_style/.

consult makes full and accurate citation essential. It's imperative that the reader understand whether the author is consulting a first-hand account (a primary source) or a secondary or tertiary source written by a scholar.

Historians cite sources with footnotes because they want to enable other people to find the sources that they used. Scholarship is ultimately a communal endeavor, with historians building on each other's work. If formatted correctly, notes provide a paper trail that others should be able to follow if they want to revisit your interpretation.

Historians use notes to provide additional information on primary sources and their biases. Sometimes, historians wish to comment further on a particular source, perhaps to provide additional detail about a source's limitations. It's often the case that the author deems this information useful but not essential to the paper's main argument and will thus provide it in a note.

Historians use notes to refer their readers to alternative viewpoints held by other historians. While historians acknowledge key contrary voices in the text of the paper, they can flesh out those different perspectives in the notes.

Historians use notes to establish their position vis-à-vis existing historiography on a particular topic. Historians build on the work of scholars who have already studied a topic. They see themselves in conversation with those scholars, some of whom might be particularly important. It can be cumbersome and confusing to a reader to flood the text of a paper with other scholars' names, so historians often use notes to spell out the ways in which their arguments connect to others' positions.[4]

For all of these reasons, historians don't find parenthetical citations adequate, largely because so little information can be conveyed in that format. It would be like asking someone to recount a story and then only allowing them to tell you the first sentence. Historians' credibility as scholars rests on fully documenting the sources from which they took their information. Notes provide much more flexibility and space for that to happen.

---

4 For more information on the use of footnotes, see "AMH 2042: How Historians Use Footnotes," posted September 3, 2014, by cliotropic, YouTube, 3 min., 52 sec., https://www.youtube.com/watch?v=qACRItfpMWI. For more information on the reasons historians use footnotes, see "Referencing," University of Colorado History Department, accessed January 19, 2024, https://www.colorado.edu/history/undergraduate/policies-and-resources/paper-guidelines/referencing.

Working with Notes

BASIC ELEMENTS OF NOTES

My students often complained that they found notes visually overwhelming, whether they were located at the bottom of the page or at the end of the paper. That may be why many students avoid reading or even glancing at notes. Right now, though, I ask that you be patient for a moment and keep an open mind.

Notes in CMS provide essential elements for source identification.[5]

Author. The author's name can be the most important piece of information that you have about a source. (If you are citing an image or a video, replace author with artist, illustrator, cartoonist, photographer, or film director.)

Title. The title is the book or article title, the title of the film or web page, and so forth. If you are citing a primary source that doesn't have a formal title, then identify what you're looking at in another way. Indicate if it's a diary entry, personal letter, advertisement, and so on.

- Titles of books, edited volumes, encyclopedias, magazines, and films go in *italics*.
- Titles of poems, articles, news stories, web pages, and book chapters go in "quotation marks." Generally, if the item can stand alone, put it in italics (such as a book). If it's something shorter that is found in a larger publication, it should be in quotation marks.

Publication information. This tells your reader who published the source. Or, if it is a primary source that you found online, you need to provide information on the organization that provided you access to that source. For a newspaper article, you'd need the name of the newspaper; for a journal article, the name of the journal.

Publication date. This is an essential piece of information that students frequently forget. Especially in the case of primary sources, dates are

---

5 For print sources, the order of the elements is generally the same. For audiovisual and online sources, however, the order of the items may vary due to a number of factors. For more details, see "Audiovisual Recordings and Other Multimedia," CMOS Formatting and Style Guide, Purdue Online Writing Lab, accessed January 19, 2025, https://owl.purdue.edu/owl/research_and_citation/chicago_manual_17th_edition.

critically important for the reader as they will demonstrate that you are referring to a source in the historical period you're studying.

Page. If you are using a source that contains page numbers, your footnote must indicate the page of the material being quoted or paraphrased. If your source does not contain page numbers (such as many web sources), be sure to provide some information that will help indicate which part of the source you've cited (such as chapter, paragraph, or location).

URL. For online sources, CMS requires the URL to be listed last. You want to be able to direct your reader to the source as efficiently as possible. Abbreviated URLs are acceptable, and more visually appealing, but be sure that readers can still locate the source easily.

EXAMPLES OF FOOTNOTES

Example A: Journal article (in online database)

First, were we to provide a citation for the journal article discussed in Chapter 6 on protest movements of the 1970s, the citation would look like this:

> 1. Simon Hall, "Protest Movements in the 1970s: The Long 1960s," *Journal of Contemporary History* 43, no. 4 (2008): 655, http://www.jstor.org/stable/40543228.

Here are the necessary elements, taken in the order outlined above:

The **author**'s name is Simon Hall, and comes first. In CMS note format, the author's name is presented in standard order (as opposed to last name, first name).

The **title** "Protest Movements in the 1970s" is the title of the article itself. Journal article titles should be placed in quotation marks.

The **publication information** is, in this case, the journal title (*Journal of Contemporary History*), volume number (43), and issue number (4). Note that the journal name is in italics.

The **date of publication** for this article is 2008.

The **page** consulted is 655.

The **URL** in this case is from JSTOR, an online journal database that provides short, stable URLs that work well for note citations. As a substitute, you could also provide the name of the commercial database in which you found the article (Academic Search or ProQuest, for instance).

Example B: An article in an edited collection

Second, let's consider an article or chapter of a larger edited volume, cited as note #19. How would this look?[6]

19. Raul Molina Mejia, "Bringing Justice to Guatemala: The Need to Confront Genocide and Other Crimes against Humanity," in *State Violence and Genocide in Latin America: The Cold Wars*, ed. Marcia Esparza, Henry R. Huttenbach, and Daniel Feierstein (Routledge, 2010), 223–24.

The **author**'s name is Raul Molina Mejia, in standard order.

The **title** of the article is in quotation marks.

The word *in* tells us that this article is found in a **larger collection** called *State Violence and Genocide in Latin America*. As a result, the **publication information** includes the editors of the collection, as well as the usual publication information we'd find for the book itself—the name of the publishing company (Routledge).

The **year** of publication of the book is 2010.

Then you find the **pages** used from the article.

The **URL** is not applicable in this case.

Example C: Primary source–presidential papers

Third, let's turn to a sample primary source found in a published collection. Note that archival or manuscript collections—which are typically not published documents—would be cited differently.

34. Dwight D. Eisenhower, "Statement by the President on Establishing the President's Committee on International Information Activities, January 26, 1953," in *Public Papers of the Presidents of the United States: Dwight D. Eisenhower, 1953* (GPO, 1960), 8.[7]

The **author**'s name is Dwight D. Eisenhower, in standard order.

The **title** of the document comes next, in quotation marks.

---

6 This example comes from Mary Lynn Rampolla, *A Pocket Guide to Writing in History*, 10th ed. (Bedford/St. Martin's, 2020), 138.

7 This example is in the 7th edition of Rampolla's *Pocket Guide* (Bedford/St. Martin's, 2012), 137.

The president's statement can be found in the **collection** title listed in italics, and the **publication information** appears subsequently in parentheses. The GPO refers to the Government Printing Office.

The document's title includes the original **date**. The publication date of the book appears in parentheses.

The **page** referenced is 8.

The **URL** is not applicable in this case.

Example D: Material from a website with an unknown author

Fourth, let's look at a website.

> 49. "Dread History: The African Diaspora, Ethiopianism, and Rastafari," Migrations in History, Smithsonian Institution, accessed October 6, 2014, https://smithsonianeducation.org/migrations/rasta/rasessay.html.[8]

The **author**'s name is unknown in this case, so you would begin with the **title** of the web page, "Dread History."

The **title** of the entire site comes next, Migrations in History.

The **sponsor of the entire site** would come next. In this case that's the Smithsonian Institution.

If there is no publication date provided for the website, include an **access date**—that is, the date on which you consulted the site.

The **page** is not applicable in this case.

The **URL** is included.

SOME ADDITIONAL RULES REGARDING NOTES

Note format. The first line of notes is always indented ½ inch from the left margin, sort of like a mini-paragraph. Notes are single-spaced.

The use of commas. Elements of footnotes are separated by commas.

Placement of notes in text. You should typically put notes at the end of a clause or a sentence, after the last word and punctuation mark. If you are quoting, the note marker (in superscript) would go after the quotation marks. If there were two quotations in one sentence, you could place a note marker in mid-sentence right after the first quotation, and the second after the second quotation.

---

8 This example is from Rampolla, 10th ed., 154.

Note frequency. Students often ask how frequently they should use footnotes. While it's not wrong to use footnotes after every sentence, it can be distracting to readers if they feel like they have to keep looking at the bottom of the page (or at the end of the paper, if you're using endnotes). One option is to use collective footnotes, which are placed at the end of each paragraph. In a collective footnote, you indicate where each piece of information in the paragraph came from, separating the elements with a semi-colon. But direct quotations should still be provided with their own note.[9]

First citations. When you complete a citation for the first time in CMS, you are required to list all the information pertinent to the citation.

Abbreviated citation formats. After the first citation of a source, CMS uses abbreviated formats. Typically, the abbreviated format requires just the author's last name, a shortened title, and the page number (if applicable). If you are using two different sources authored by the same person, make sure that it's easy to tell which of the sources the citation is referring to. Shortened forms for the sources A to D cited above would appear like this:

Hall, "Protest Movements," 656.
Mejia, "Bringing Justice," 225.
Eisenhower, "Statement by the President," 9.
Smithsonian Institution,[10] "Dread History."

The use of ibid. Up until the 16th edition, *Chicago Manual of Style* recommended using the Latin abbreviation "ibid." when citing the same source in numerical sequence. Later editions of *CMS* (beginning with the 17th), however, discourage the use of ibid., and instead recommend the shortened citation format, which appears above. If you cite the same work two or more times, and no other sources from that author are utilized, you could abbreviate the citation further to include only the author or title and page number.[11]

Anticipate having to improvise. Recognize that even though citation models will help you to figure out how to cite the vast majority of the sources you are using for your paper, you may still need to improvise for one or two of the less conventional types of sources you encounter. While there are

9 "Referencing," University of Colorado History Department.

10 Since there is no author provided for this website, the sponsoring organization (the Smithsonian) is substituted in the abbreviated version.

11 "Chicago Manual of Style 17th Edition," Purdue Online Writing Lab, accessed November 22, 2024, https://owl.purdue.edu/owl/research_and_citation/chicago_manual_17th_edition.

plenty of documentation guides out there, it's sometimes difficult to find explicit guidelines on every type of source you find. Here's my advice for these frustrating moments: The most important thing is to include all the information in the citation that is necessary to locate the source, and to try to be as consistent with formatting as possible. There are few things more frustrating for your instructor than seeing the formatting style change for every note, or finding that half the information is missing.

MAKING SENSE OF NOTES

Let's complete our attempt to demystify footnotes by seeing if we can unscramble an actual series of footnotes found in a chapter of a historical text. The numbers below correspond to each footnote listed.

Sample Footnotes

1. *Gateway to History*, 1938. Quoted in Louis Starr, "Oral History," in *Oral History: An Interdisciplinary Anthology*, ed. David K. Dunaway and Willa K. Baum (American Association for State and Local History, 1984), 8.
2. Quoted in Robert P. Swierenga, ed., *Quantification in American History* (Atheneum, 1970), xi.
3. Richard N. Goodwin, *Remembering America* (Harper and Row, 1988), 267–68.
4. Paul F. Boller, Jr., *Presidential Anecdotes* (Penguin, 1981), 307.
5. Quoted in Boller, *Presidential Anecdotes,* 309.
6. Goodwin, *Remembering America,* 260.
7. As it turns out, long after President Johnson left office the public learned that many of his private phone conversations had not been lost after all. For years, even before he became president, LBJ kept records of his phone calls, first by having an aide take shorthand notes, and then by tape recorder. Johnson originally intended that the recordings be locked away until the year 2023, but they were released early. See Michael Beschloss's *Taking Charge: The Johnson White House Tapes, 1963–1964* (Simon and Schuster, 1997), and *Reaching for Glory: Lyndon Johnson's Secret White House Tapes, 1964–1965* (Simon and Schuster, 2001). These tapes actually dramatize the point made above: they are a very rare exception to the reality that the great majority of phone messages are lost to historians forever. And, if LBJ had had his way, no historian would have listened to those tapes until well into the twenty-first century.
8. Dunaway and Baum, *Oral History*, xix.
9. Barbara Tuchman, "Distinguishing the Significant from the Insignificant," in Dunaway and Baum, *Oral History*, 76.
10. For example, Cullom Davis, Kathryn Back, and Kay MacLean, *Oral History: From Tape to Type* (American Library Association, 1977); Thad Sitton, George L. Mehaffy, and O.L. Davis, Jr., *Oral History: A Guide for Teachers (and Others)* (University of Texas Press, 1983); James Hoopes, *Oral History: An Introduction for Students* (University of North Carolina Press, 1979). Section V ("Oral History and Schools") of Dunaway and Baum (1984) is also valuable. The bibliography of this work lists a number of additional oral history manuals.

Source: Adapted from Conal Furay and Michael J. Salevouris, *The Methods and Skills of History: A Practical Guide*, 3rd ed. (Harlan Davidson, 2010), 165–69.

1. Whenever you see the phrase "quoted in" in footnotes, the author is using a passage that is quoted in the source they are referencing. The first footnote quotes a source originally found in a book called *Gateway to History*, published in 1938. The reason the citation does not contain an author (just the title) is because the name of the author who wrote *Gateway to History* was included in the text. Since the *Gateway to History* book is an abbreviated citation, we know that the authors have included a full citation at an earlier point in the paper.

   This quotation was found in the article by Louis Starr called "Oral History," on page 8 of a collection edited by Dunaway and Baum. This collection has not yet been cited in the paper, because the full citation information is provided.
2. A quotation in the text is taken from p. xi of a book edited by Robert Swierenga. This is the first time the Swierenga book is cited as a full citation is provided. We don't have the original source of the quotation, even though that was provided for the first quotation cited in note 1.
3. This note directs us to another source cited for the first time, a book called *Remembering America*.
4. The authors introduce a new source, Boller's *Presidential Anecdotes*.
5. The authors cite a quotation used on a different page in Boller's book.
6. The authors again use the source originally cited in note 3, *Remembering America*.
7. The authors begin this note with the phrase "As it turns out," suggesting that the insight shared in the footnote came to the authors' attention after the original article was written. Here, we learn that President Johnson's valuable telephone calls, which we thought were lost to history, were actually recorded. Several studies have been written on the content of those conversations, including the books by Michael Beschloss listed here. The existence of these tapes is something highly unusual and reinforces the main point that such exceptions to the rule are quite rare.
8. The authors again refer to the collection cited in note 1. We have an abbreviated note because the full citation has already been provided. From the page number provided (xix), it seems that this is a reference to an introduction written by the editors of the collection.

9. The authors cite Barbara Tuchman's article, which is also found in the collection originally cited in note 1. The authors are able to cite just the author, title of the article, and page, while providing the name of the edited volume. Again, that is because the publication information for the volume was provided in note 1.
10. When a note begins with "For example," we can assume that the authors are providing a list of sources that they allude to in the text itself. This is clearly a list of books about using oral history in a research project. This is a great example of a note intended to provide supplemental information for a student who wanted to learn more about a topic. It would be quite overwhelming to a reader to see all of this information listed in the text, so the authors use a footnote to serve the purpose.

The Bibliography

If notes are already so detailed and provide all citation information for the sources consulted, why are bibliographies necessary in history papers? That's a fair question. For one thing, there might be other sources that you read along the way that are not included in the footnotes. That's because you almost never cite every source you have consulted in the course of writing a paper due to space limitations. It's also much easier to navigate a properly formatted bibliography than it is to peruse a paper's notes.

Here are some points that will help you to distinguish the bibliography from notes in your paper:

- A bibliography is a list of all the sources consulted for the paper, be they articles, books, or websites. The sources are listed in alphabetical order by author's or editor's last name, or by the first key word of a title if an author or editor is unknown. Bibliography entries are never numbered.
- While you may include some sources consulted during your research that you didn't actually cite in the paper itself, you should not engage in "padding" the bibliography with sources that you did not find helpful or relevant to your topic.
- The bibliography is placed at the end of the paper, after the endnotes (if you are using them).

- Bibliography entries contain the same basic information that exists in a note citation. The formatting is slightly different, however. First, elements are separated by periods, not commas. The author's name is listed in reverse order as "last name, first name." A full page range for a journal article is provided in a bibliography, but not a note. A page range for a chapter or article in a book is not required in a bibliography, and individual pages cited also do not appear.
- Bibliographies feature a "reverse indent" for each new entry, meaning the entry's first line starts at the left margin of the paper, but each subsequent line is indented ½ inch.
- Bibliography entries are single-spaced within individual entries.
- If you use more than one source written by a single author, list the author name for each title. List the individual titles in alphabetical order.[12]

Note vs. Bibliography Formats

In the chart below, you'll find a comparison of note and bibliography formats.

Summary of Differences between Note and Bibliography Formats in CMS

CRITERION	NOTES	BIBLIOGRAPHIES
What is included	Citations are included for each source consulted in the body of the paper.	Entries are included for each source useful to you in the research stages, even if not explicitly mentioned in the paper.
Placement in paper	Notes appear at the bottom of each page (footnotes) or at the end of the paper, before the bibliography (endnotes).	The bibliography appears at the end of the paper. The bibliography page is numbered as the next page after the last page of text.

12 "CMOS NB Sample Paper," Purdue Online Writing Lab, accessed November 22, 2024, https://owl.purdue.edu/owl/research_and_citation. It is helpful to look at a sample paper such as this one when completing your own assignment to make sure you have the formatting correctly done.

Numbered or alphabetical	Notes are numbered and placed in sequential order throughout the paper.	Bibliography entries are placed in alphabetical order by the author's last name. They are not numbered.
Indentation	The first line of each note is indented a half-inch.	Each new bibliography entry starts at the left margin; second and subsequent lines are indented a half-inch (a reverse indent).
Spacing	Notes are single-spaced. A blank line is inserted between each note entry.	Bibliography entries are single-spaced. A blank line is inserted between each bibliography entry.
Author's name	Authors' names appear in standard order of first name last name.	First author's name appears in reverse order (last name, first name). Second and subsequent authors' names are in standard order.
Element separation	Elements of note citations are separated by commas.	Elements of bibliography entries are separated by periods.
Pages	Only the page utilized is included in the note.	The full page range of a journal article is included in the bibliography. The page range of a book chapter is not required.
Multiple uses of the same author	Full entry for a source appears once. Use abbreviated source citation (author, title, page) afterwards.	Use the author's name in each instance (last, first), listing titles in alphabetical order.

Note and Bibliography Entry Models

In the chart below, you'll see format models for frequently used sources in research papers. In the samples listed here, "first name last name" always applies to the author, unless otherwise indicated. If "ed." appears, then the editor's name is placed there. If "trans." appears, include the name of the translator.

SOURCE TYPE	N/B	A PARTIAL LIST OF CHICAGO MANUAL OF STYLE FORMAT MODELS FOR NOTES (N) AND BIBLIOGRAPHY (B)*
Book	**N**	1. First Name Last Name, *Title in Italics* (Publisher, year of publication), page.
	B	Last Name, First Name. *Title in Italics.* Publisher, year of publication.
E-Book	**N**	1. First Name Last Name, *Title in Italics* (Publisher, year of publication), chap. # or loc. #, E-book platform.
	B	Last Name, First Name. *Title in Italics.* Publisher, year of publication. E-book platform.
Book with 2 authors	**N**	1. First Name Last Name and First Name Last Name, *Title in Italics* (Publisher, year of publication), page.
	B	Last Name, First name, and First Name Last Name. *Title in Italics.* Publisher, year of publication.
Book with 3–6 authors	**N**	In the note, use et al. (Latin for "and others") after the first author's name.
	B	List all authors' names in the bibliography entry.
Edited book (no author provided)	**N**	1. First Name Last Name, ed., *Title in Italics* (Publisher, year of publication), page.
	B	Last Name, First Name, ed. *Title in Italics.* Publisher, year of publication.
Edited work with an author	**N**	1. First name Last Name, *Title in Italics*, ed. First Name Last Name (Publisher, year of publication), page.
	B	Last Name, First Name. *Title in Italics.* Edited by First Name Last Name. Publisher, year of publication.
Translated work	**N**	1. First Name Last name, *Title in Italics*, trans. First Name Last Name (Publisher, year of publication), page.
	B	Last Name, First Name. *Title in Italics.* Translated by First Name Last Name. Publisher, year of publication.
Foreword, preface, introduction or afterword	**N**	1. First name Last Name, introduction to *Title in Italics* (Publisher, year of publication), page.
	B	Last Name, First Name. Introduction to *Title in Italics.* Publisher, year of publication.
Article or chapter in an edited work (anthology)	**N**	1. First Name Last Name of Article Author, "Article Title in Quotation Marks," in *Book Title in Italics*, ed. First Name Last Name of Editor (Publisher, year of publication), page.
	B	Last Name, First Name. "Article Title in Quotation Marks." In *Book Title in Italics*, edited by First Name Last Name of Editor. Publisher, year of publication.
Letter in published collection	**N**	1. Sender's First Name Last Name to Recipient's First Name Last Name, date, in *Name of Anthology in Italics*, ed. First Name Last Name (Publisher, year of publication), page.
	B	Sender's Last Name, First Name. Sender's First Name Last Name to Recipient's First Name Last Name, Date. In *Name of Anthology in Italics*, edited by First Name Last Name. Publisher, year of publication.

2+ letters from the same collection	**N**	Same as above (letter in published collection).
	B	Only list the collection, not the individual letters.
Illustration, table or map (visual source) in larger book	**N**	1. Creator's First Name Last Name, *Title of Item in Italics* (illustration, table, or map), in Compiler's First Name, Last Name, *Name of Volume in Italics* (Publisher, year of publication), page #, figure # (or table #).
	B	Creator's Last Name, First name. *Name of Item in Italics* (illustration, table, or map). In Compiler's First Name, Last Name. *Name of Volume in Italics*. Publisher, year of publication, page #s.
Source quoted in another source (acknowledge both the original source and where you found the information)	**N**	1. First Name Last Name of quoted author, *Title of Original Source* (Publisher, year of publication), page, quoted in First Name Last Name, *Title of Source Containing Quote* (Publisher, year of publication), page.
	B	Last Name, First Name of quoted author. *Title of Original Source*. Publisher, year of publication. Quoted in First Name Last Name, *Title of Source Containing Quote.* Publisher, year of publication.
Dictionary or encyclopedia (omit publication information, volume and pages)	**N**	1: *Name of Encyclopedia*, no. of edition (year), under "title of entry." 2. *Title of Dictionary*, no. of edition (year), under "title of entry."
	B	Entries from well-known encyclopedias and dictionaries are not listed in bibliographies. If you cite an entry from a specialized encyclopedia, use the model for a chapter in an edited book on p. 159.
Article in online journal	**N**	1. First Name Last Name, "Title of Journal Article," *Title of Journal* Vol. #, issue # (Year): page cited, DOI or URL.** **EXAMPLE:** 1. Marjo Uutela, "Narrowing Finland's Cold War Neutrality Narrative," *Journal of Contemporary History* 60, no. 1 (2025): 64–79, https://doi.org/10.1177/00220094241306984.
	B	Last Name, First Name. "Title of Journal Article." *Title of Journal* Vol. #, issue # (Year): page range. DOI or URL. **EXAMPLE:** Uutela, Marjo. "Narrowing Finland's Cold War Neutrality Narrative." *Journal of Contemporary History* 60, no. 1 (2025): 64–79. https://doi.org/10.1177/00220094241306984.
Journal article from database	**N**	1. First Name Last Name, "Title of Journal Article," *Title of Journal* Vol. #, issue # (Year): page cited, Stable URL or Database Name.***
	B	Last Name, First Name. "Title of Journal Article." *Title of Journal* Vol. #, issue # (Year): page range. Stable URL or Database Name.
Article in an online magazine	**N**	1. First Name Last Name, "Title of Article," *Name of Magazine*, Date of issue, URL.
	B	Last Name, First Name. "Title of Article." *Name of Magazine*, Date of issue. URL.

Article in an online newspaper	**N**	1. First Name Last name, "Title of Article," *Name of Newspaper*, Date of Article, URL.
	B	Last Name, First Name. "Title of Article." *Name of Newspaper*, Date of Article. URL.
Film, Television, or video	**N**	1. *Title of Recording*, directed by First Name Last Name, aired Date and Year, on Channel (Studio, Year). **EXAMPLE:** 1. *Game Change*, directed by Jay Roach, aired March 10, 2012, on HBO (HBO, 2012).
	B	*Title of Recording.* Directed by First Name Last Name. Aired Date and Year, on Channel. Studio, Year. **EXAMPLE:** *Game Change.* Directed by Jay Roach. Aired March 10, 2012, on HBO. HBO, 2012.
YouTube video	**N**	1. "Title of Video," posted Month, day, year, by [YouTube Channel], YouTube, running time, URL. **EXAMPLE:** 1. "Library Orientation Video 2024," posted August 20, 2024, by shapirolibrary, YouTube, 4 min., 11 sec., https://www.youtube.com/watch?v=qLAELKOVzJ0.
	B	"Title of Video." Posted Month, day, year, by [YouTube Channel]. YouTube, running time. URL. **EXAMPLE:** "Library Orientation Video 2024." Posted August 20, 2024, by shapirolibrary. YouTube, 4 min., 11 sec. https://www.youtube.com/watch?v=qLAELKOVzJ0.****
Personal interview	**N**	1. Interviewee First Name Last Name, interview by First Name Last Name, place and date of interview.
	B	Do not include personal interviews in the bibliography.
Personal email	**N**	1. Source First Name Last Name, email message to author, date of email.
	B	Do not include personal emails in the bibliography.
Web page	**N**	1. "Title of Page," Title of Site, sponsor of the site, date of publication or revision (or date of access), URL.
	B	Not usually included in the bibliography

* All of these models are adapted from Mary Lynn Rampolla, *A Pocket Guide to Writing in History*, 10th ed. (Bedford/St. Martin's, 2021), 127–55.

** A DOI is a Digital Object Identifier that provides a permanent web address for an article.

*** For articles found in databases, list the URL only if the database provides a stable form. If it doesn't, list just the name of the database (such as LexisNexis). CMS typically does not require access dates.

**** This example came from "FAQ: How Do I Cite a YouTube Video in Chicago Style?" FAQ, Southern New Hampshire University Shapiro Library, accessed November 6, 2024, https://libanswers.snhu.edu/faq/48007. If you knew the precise author of the YouTube video, the name of the person would be included prior to the title.

Use Citation Generators with Care

I hear what you're saying. This chapter looks pretty unnecessary, right? Why do I have to learn the details of a particular citation style when there is so much citation software available? While I don't dispute that these resources are incredibly helpful, many students turn enthusiastically to software and refuse to take responsibility for making sure that the citations generated are formatted correctly. They copy and paste citations in their notes and bibliographies without even looking at them to make sure they are free of errors. Note that you need to enter the information perfectly for these sites, and even if you do, some generators make errors in producing the citation. Moreover, not all sources are the easiest to cite. Bottom line: You must check that what comes out of the citation generator is correct—and fix the mistakes. If you don't, you're the one at fault—not the software.[13]

See Online Companion Exercise 13
sites.broadviewpress.com/puzzle/chapter-13

13 See, for instance, "Using Citation Generators Responsibly," Research and Citation, Purdue Online Writing Lab, accessed November 23, 2024, https://owl.purdue.edu/owl/research_and_citation.

CHAPTER 14

Quoting in a Historical Paper

Some students really love to quote, and to a fault. Let's get one thing straight from the start: quoting too much in a historical essay is a bad idea. When I saw a paper with too many quotes (particularly long block quotes), this is the message the writer was sending me, loud and clear: "I am trying to fill space to reach the suggested word length." Sometimes, I even went so far as to highlight all the quotations and hand the paper back to the student with a comment regarding how much had *actually* been written by the student. (That's not nice—I'll admit it. But it's an important lesson to learn.)

Quotations should never be space-fillers, as your instructor will see through that strategy right away. Using quotations as a crutch is precisely the opposite of what you should be doing. The vast majority of the writing in your history paper should be your own words. Paraphrase and summary should be your first choice, with quoting an option only when certain conditions apply.

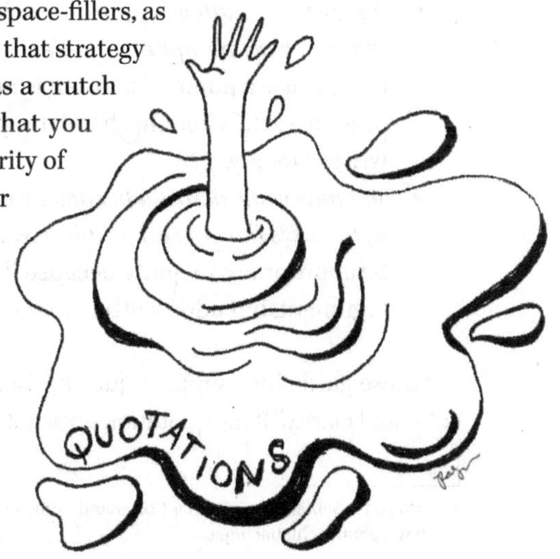

A very smart historian has some rules for historical writing, framed as a set of commandments. Rule #7 reads, "Thou shalt use quotations sparingly and judiciously, only for color and clarity; if thou must quote, quotations should not break the flow of thine own language and logic, and thy text should make clear whom thou art quoting."[1] Though originally written almost thirty years ago, this "commandment" still rings true today. Let's break it down into a few smaller segments, each of which this chapter will address:

- Use quotations carefully, and only to add a degree of precision or flavor to your writing that you cannot accomplish otherwise.
- Integrate quotations fully into your own writing.
- Be clear as to whom you are quoting.

When You Should Quote

Historians use pretty strict guidelines when selecting quotations. Here are a few criteria to help you determine when a quotation may be appropriate:

- *The text of a primary source supports your argument well.* Let's say you are trying to make a point, and you find an outstanding quotation in one of your sources that illustrates what you are saying. Rather than trying to paraphrase the source, you decide to insert a selection into the text of your paper. It brings the voice of the historical actor into your writing.
- *A secondary author supports or refutes your argument so eloquently that you can't paraphrase it adequately.* Sometimes it is hard to paraphrase a point a historian is making and do justice to the original text. When this happens, you may want to quote the writer directly.
- *You may come across a particular phrase or expression that a writer uses that you especially like.* In this circumstance it may be appropriate to quote because it not only contributes to your argument, but adds a little more spice to your language.

These guidelines support quoting "sparingly and judiciously, only for color and clarity." If the quotation does not specifically serve your argument,

1 Theron F. Schlabach, "The Ten Commandments of Good Historical Writing," 1996, http://www.geraldschlabach.net/.

it does not belong in your paper. I would recommend that you choose your quotations based on these rules and include those you intend to use in your sentence outline. Be sure *not* to include any other quotations unless they meet one of the above three conditions.

The important thing to remember is that this is *your* paper, not someone else's. Not only does overloading your paper with quotations suggest that you are trying to fill space, it undermines your credibility as an author and thinker. If in every other sentence, you're inserting someone else's voice, the reader will come to believe that you don't really know what you're talking about and are relying on quotations to hide your own lack of expertise or original thinking. Quoting excessively means ceding to the people you are quoting the authority that, in your paper, should rightfully belong to you.

Integrating Quotations into Text

Once you have made sure that the quotations you've selected will serve your argument in a particular way, you'll need to figure out how to incorporate them into your writing. Below, we'll go over a few techniques to help you do this properly. In practicing these techniques, keep a few main objectives in mind:

- *Anchor your quotation.* Your quotation needs to be used in support of a larger point that you're making in your paper. If you don't do this properly, your reader will wonder why you're quoting in the first place, as your quotation will seem to have been inserted randomly. *Anchoring* implies prefacing your quotation with some introductory words and explaining why it's relevant. A properly anchored quotation does not interrupt the flow of the author's prose and makes sense to the reader.
- *Cite your source.* You should also be sure to provide a citation for the source you're quoting, in the form of a footnote. This seems

obvious, but students frequently get into trouble if they're not careful when doing this.[2]

In order to illustrate the techniques that you should use when incorporating quotations into your writing, we will rely on a sample historical text (our "original") and keep referring back to it for the examples provided below.

Below, you'll see five strategies for integrating a quotation into your writing so that it is properly anchored, as defined above. Remember, "[Q]uotations should not break the flow of thine own language and logic."

Primary Source

Images of the 1950s are distinct: white middle-class families, suburban homes, backyard barbecues, big American cars with tail fins, Little League and Girl Scouts, peace, prosperity, and harmony. So, too, the images of the 1960s: civil rights sit-ins, urban violence, antiwar demonstrations, Black Power salutes, hippie love-ins, draft card burnings, death and destruction in Vietnam, police riots in Chicago, obscenities, hostilities, killings at Kent State and Jackson State universities.

These decades stand in marked contrast in the collective memory, each reduced to recollections distilled from media imagery and popular stereotypes. The periods recede into history, reflections of the dominant values of their eras rather than accurate representations of the complexity of their times: the harmonious 1950s; the turbulent 1960s. We remember the eras in stark opposition, in snapshots that symbolize values and aspirations unrelated to one another.

As scholars look back at these eras, however, they understand them as complex and interrelated. The obvious tensions and anxieties of postwar America—the cold war, fear of the atom bomb, McCarthyism and the specter of the witch-hunt—are easily recalled; they undermine notions of a calm and peaceful era. Questions about race and gender have further demonstrated that the 1950s were not nearly so harmonious for minorities and women. We now understand more clearly the complexities of family life, the pressures on men and women resulting from rigid gender roles, the large numbers of Americans—of all races—who felt left out of the suburban dream of the good life. All these suggest an era far more anxious, questioning, and discordant than do bland images of postwar bliss.

Source: Alexander Bloom and Wini Breines, "'Past as Prologue': The 1950s as an Introduction to the 1960s," in *'Takin' It to the Streets': A Sixties Reader*, ed. Alexander Bloom and Wini Breines (Oxford University Press, 2003), 1.

2 These points and the strategies presented below come from "Paraphrases and Quotes," University of Iowa History Writing Center, accessed November 23, 2024, https://history.uiowa.edu/resources/history-writing-center.

1. Use an introductory sentence that sets up the quotation.

> Our memories of the 1950s and the 1960s call up drastically different periods in American history: "We remember the eras in stark opposition, in snapshots that symbolize values and aspirations unrelated to one another." [note]

In this example, the quotation supports the point made in the introductory portion of the sentence and uses eloquent language to reinforce the author's main message. The quotation is prefaced with a colon.

2. Use signal words that tell your reader that you are citing a source:

> Even though we remember the 1950s and 1960s as completely different eras, historians have identified points of continuity between the two decades. As Alexander Bloom and Wini Breines explain, "scholars ... understand them as complex and interrelated." [note]

In this example, the word "explain" tells the reader where my words have stopped and the quoted authors' words begin. I have provided the proper context so that the quotation makes sense. Bloom and Breines's point about the relationship between these decades helps to clarify my point that the 1950s and 1960s have more in common than might be suggested by the ideas about these decades that have become entrenched in American culture. I have also used an *ellipsis* (...) between the words "scholars" and "understand" so that the sentence makes sense. Ellipses (the plural of ellipsis) tell the reader that the original source contains additional text at that point, but that I have left it out for the quoted material to read well grammatically. Authors frequently use ellipses in order to isolate the most important parts of quoted text. (More on the use of ellipses below.)

Here's another version of the example above:

> Even though we remember the 1950s and 1960s as completely different eras, historians have identified points of continuity. As Alexander Bloom and Wini Breines explain, "scholars ... understand [these decades] as complex and interrelated." [note]

Here, I've provided the words "these decades" in brackets instead of using the word "them." This helps me be certain that the reader knows what "them" refers to in the quotation I have cited.

3. Incorporate a portion of a quotation into your own writing.

> Regardless of race or socioeconomic level, American families of the 1950s experienced domestic tensions. Recent scholarship "suggest[s] an era far more anxious, questioning, and discordant than do bland images of postwar bliss." [note]

Though I have not used a signal verb, per se, in this example, it is clear where I am transitioning from my own language to the point that Bloom and Breines are making. I have modified the text I am quoting with brackets so that "suggest[s]" agrees with the singular noun "scholarship," even though in the original it reads "suggest."

4. Break up a quotation into two parts, placing the authors' names in the middle.

> Our memories of the 1950s and 1960s differ from historians' perspectives. Even though "[w]e remember the eras in stark opposition [to one another]," Bloom and Breines explain, scholars "understand them as complex and interrelated." [note]

These quotations are actually from two different sentences in the secondary source. Placing them in the same sentence of my paper highlights the difference in perspective that historians bring to the study of these decades.[3]

5. Frame block quotations so that they are fully integrated into your text.

> As Wini Breines and Alexander Bloom explain, we have become accustomed to remembering the 1950s and the 1960s in starkly different ways:

3 More discussion of this technique can be found at "Quotations," Writing Center at UNC Chapel Hill, accessed November 23, 2024, https://writingcenter.unc.edu/tips-and-tools/quotations/.

> Those decades stand in marked contrast in the collective memory, each reduced to recollections distilled from media imagery and popular stereotypes. The periods recede into history, reflections of the dominant values of their eras rather than accurate representations of the complexity of the times: the harmonious 1950s; the turbulent 1960s. We remember the eras in stark opposition, in snapshots that symbolize values and aspirations unrelated to one another. [note]

Our memories of the 1950s and 1960s have been translated into catch phrases that help us to quickly characterize each decade. As a result, we sacrifice historical accuracy for easy sound bites.

In this example, I have chosen a block quotation from the authors that I have indented one-half inch from the text due to its length. I have not included quotation marks because visually it is now clear that I am quoting someone. However, I have included a citation at the end of the quotation. Just as important, I have introduced the quotation and have followed it with a brief summary of the authors' main point. Similarly, had I chosen to quote a primary source at such length, I would need to include analysis and interpretation of the source so that it was clear what that source was contributing to my argument.

Imagine for a moment if I had *not* included the explanation of the block quotation, but had simply gone on to a separate topic without indicating why I had devoted so much space to Breines and Bloom's points on historical memory. This omission would leave my reader without a clue as to where I was going. Hopefully by now, it's clear why this doesn't work. Writing instructors call this "quoting and running," as you've moved on before fully taking care of your responsibility as an author.

Strategies for Quoting Clearly and Accurately

Students frequently make mistakes when citing their sources. They misquote authors by deleting an important word, forget footnotes, or otherwise misrepresent the original. One of the most frequent mistakes I found was that students forget the closing quotation marks, leaving the reader wondering where the author's voice takes over. I strongly recommend comparing your quotation to the original text after your paper is done to make sure that you have not inadvertently made an error.

In order to make sure you represent your sources accurately, there are a few rules to keep in mind.[4] Here is another passage from the next page of the source used earlier, "Past as Prologue":

Primary Source

Memory compresses the past, so that it seems that life was pacific at one moment and the nation exploded in the next. Deeper analysis of the two eras reveals continuities between them. At the simplest level, political activities such as the civil rights movement began in the 1950s. Little Leaguers and Girl Scouts of the fifties grew up to become the college students of the sixties. Unhappiness over the prescribed roles white postwar brides were asked to play in their "suburban utopias" was a shared experience for many fifties housewives and proved a crucial impetus for the women's movement of the late sixties. Younger women sought new roles beyond limits that had been drawn for their mothers.

Source: Alexander Bloom and Wini Breines, "'Past as Prologue': The 1950s as an Introduction to the 1960s," in *'Takin' It to the Streets': A Sixties Reader*, ed. Alexander Bloom and Wini Breines (Oxford University Press, 2003), 2.

- If your original source contains a quotation within it, use single quotation marks to represent that quotation.

As Breines and Bloom argue, young women in the 1950s felt frustrated by the limitations imposed upon them because of their gender. They were dissatisfied with "the prescribed roles ... [they] were asked to play in their 'suburban utopias.'" [note]

Since the authors place "suburban utopias" in (double) quotation marks in the original source, I use single quotation marks within my quotation to indicate how it originally appeared.

- Use an ellipsis in your quotation [...] to indicate that you are leaving out a few words of text from the original source. You can do this as long as whatever you've left out does not change the meaning of the original.

4 The strategies below are also from "Quotations," Writing Center at UNC Chapel Hill.

Breines and Bloom point out that the 1950s and the 1960s were decades that had a great deal in common: "Deeper analysis ... reveals continuities between them." [note]

- Do not use an ellipsis at the beginning or end of the quoted phrase in your paper.

INCORRECT:
Breines and Bloom assert "... Memory compresses the past." [note]
INCORRECT:
Breines and Bloom assert "Memory compresses the past ..." [note]
CORRECT:
As Breines and Bloom assert, "Memory compresses the past." [note]

- When you are quoting material, and wish to indicate that you are leaving out material at the end of a sentence or clause, leave the comma or period.

Breines and Bloom complicate our oversimplified memory of the 1950s and 1960s when they write, "Deeper analysis of the two eras reveals continuities." They continue, "[P]olitical activities such as the civil rights movement began in the 1950s. ... Girl Scouts of the fifties grew up to become the college students of the sixties." [note]

If I were referring specifically to women's experiences in my essay, I might have reason to focus on the authors' references to Girl Scouts, and omit mention of "Little Leaguers." The initial period after "1950s" in the quoted passage indicates that the sentence ended there in the original source. An ellipsis immediately afterwards suggests the omission of a word, phrase, or one or more sentences.

- Do not misrepresent the meaning of a passage by leaving out essential information.

Breines and Bloom argued "that life was pacific at one moment and the nation exploded in the next." [note]

This sentence does not fairly represent what the authors are saying in this passage. It leaves out the larger context, making it seem as though Breines and Bloom intended the opposite of what they wrote.

Quoting properly takes practice. This brief list of guidelines is not intended to be exhaustive by any means. Rather, my hope is that as a student new to writing history papers in college, you'll appreciate the fact that incorporating quotations wisely is something that takes time, patience, and care. It's not something that you can trust to go smoothly at 3:00 a.m. before the paper is due.

See Online Companion Exercise 14
sites.broadviewpress.com/puzzle/chapter-14

CHAPTER 15

Avoiding Plagiarism and Using Artificial Intelligence

Plagiarism has become a bigger problem in the last two decades because of the wide variety of sources available on the internet—including, most recently, generative AI platforms such as ChatGPT. The ease with which students can access online articles makes it very tempting to cut and paste someone else's writing into a Word document and pass it off as one's own. Students can also buy papers from "paper mills," online businesses that sell completed essays to students at high prices. And, of course, it is now

possible to ask ChatGPT or another such AI platform to generate an entire essay on any topic under the sun. (I will say more about generative AI and its use at the end of this chapter.) Ultimately, it doesn't matter where you get your paper from if you didn't write it yourself. If you pass off someone (or, in the case of AI, something) else's work as your own, it's plagiarism.

You don't want to be charged with plagiarism in college, as that charge (if upheld) would seriously impact your academic standing and will become part of your permanent record. Colleges and universities have strict policies for penalizing students who have plagiarized, and professors often list their own policies in their course syllabus.[1] These consequences could range from a failing grade on an assignment, or for a class, to suspension from the institution for multiple violations. As an instructor, I liked nothing less than having to fail a student for plagiarizing. Confronting a student suspected of plagiarism was equally unpleasant.

As a college student, you've undoubtedly heard about the importance of avoiding plagiarism. First-year orientation programs devote considerable time to it. What I found to be the case over and over again, though, was that students and their instructors didn't necessarily define plagiarism the same way. Instructors assumed that students had already been taught everything they need to know in high school. Students, on the other hand, had a wide range of ideas of what constitutes plagiarism, which may or may not overlap with the instructor's. My goal in this chapter is to establish some common ground on what plagiarism actually is, why it happens, and how to avoid it.

Defining Plagiarism

According to the Council of Writing Program Administrators, "plagiarism occurs when a writer deliberately uses someone else's language, ideas or other original (not common-knowledge) material without acknowledging its source."[2] The word "deliberately" is important here, because it implies the intention to mislead a reader on the question of authorship. A related but less serious problem (theoretically) has to do with *misuse of sources*, which can be defined as "carelessly or inadequately citing ideas and words

1 These policies are often included under the umbrella of academic integrity.

2 "Defining and Avoiding Plagiarism: The WPA Statement on Best Practices," Council of Writing Program Administrators, December 30, 2019, http://www.wpacouncil.org.

borrowed from another source."[3] "Misuse of sources" suggests the student did not *intend* to take credit for another's words, but instead made mistakes in citation, which may have misled a reader on the issue of authorship.

I should add that when we're talking about plagiarism, it does not matter if the assignment is a short homework assignment, a formal paper, or an in-class presentation. I had some students who assumed that if they handed in a homework assignment that included questions from an assigned reading they could simply copy word for word from the author's text. I had other students who made a poster presentation and thought that that format made the rules of academic integrity less applicable. They were wrong. The point is that anything you submit—whether graded or ungraded, formal or informal—needs to contain proper documentation, regardless of what it is. Copying from an assigned reading—even if your professor is familiar with the source—is never acceptable.

At first glance, it appears that these two actions (*plagiarism* and *misuse of sources*) should be entirely distinct from one another. How is the misuse of sources, which stems from an unintentional error on a student's part, the same as plagiarism? In theory, they are quite different types of mistakes. The problem is that in practice they often overlap. A student's improper citation techniques can easily make an instructor *think* a student has plagiarized even when they didn't mean to do so. Improper citation causes a great deal of confusion, forcing the student to have to explain to an instructor that their intentions were good. Instructors then wonder if the student is being entirely honest or is trying to avoid taking responsibility for the mistake. The problems that result from relying on good intentions (alone) are significant, leaving both you as the student and the instructor in a very tough spot. The only way to prevent this sticky situation altogether is to learn proper citation skills.

Why Students Plagiarize

As you try to hone your skills in this area, let's first look at some of the situations that cause students to plagiarize. You'll want to be aware of these traps so you can avoid them in the course of your college career.

3 "Defining and Avoiding Plagiarism," Council of Writing Program Administrators.

1. *A student has procrastinated, and panics at the last minute.* Often, plagiarism results from not starting the assignment early enough to get the work done. A student lacks the time to complete the assignment properly or get their questions answered. With a matter of hours left before the deadline, the student plagiarizes in order to have something to hand in.
2. *A student lacks confidence to complete the assignment adequately, or does not fully understand the assignment.* In this situation, a student may have looked at the assignment early enough, but does not get the help needed to do it properly. The instructions may be unclear, or the student lacks the appropriate background. The student may feel uncomfortable admitting that they're in this position, especially if the deadline is now approaching. Fearing a bad grade, the student resorts to plagiarism in order to have something to submit.
3. *A student thinks that it is not worth the time to do the assignment properly.* A student may find a class boring or not relevant to their interests, and wishes they didn't have to take the class in the first place. They have the same attitude for most of the assignments on the course syllabus. They decide that it's easier to just buy a paper from a website or use AI to generate one than to take the time to do it themselves.[4]

All three of these situations imply an intent to plagiarize and will likely result in pretty severe consequences for the student. Chances are that in cases 1 and 2 the student wanted to complete the assignment properly, but panicked at the last minute. In case 3, the student seems to have wanted to save time and effort by avoiding the work, or seems to have believed the work to be not worth doing.

The solution to the problems in 1 and 2 is easy. Start early, ask questions, and make sure you have a plan of action that is manageable in the time allotted. Believe me, your instructor would much rather clarify instructions, or meet with you to answer questions, than have to address the issue of plagiarism. If you are really having trouble and express your concern well in advance, you may be able to secure an extension for your assignment.

4 "Defining and Avoiding Plagiarism," Council of Writing Program Administrators. The CWPA provides a broader explanation of the reasons students plagiarize. Here, I have presented the scenarios I encountered most frequently as an instructor.

But for case 3, the student should be advised that it might be harder to get away with this scheme than it used to be. Due to the increasing frequency with which students turn to paper mills or AI in order to get assignments written, instructors have come up with some new techniques to determine if students have written a paper themselves. Sometimes, instructors will interview the student about the paper's content, asking questions about conceptual development, sources, etc. You can't really answer those questions if you didn't do the work. This is a pretty easy way to determine if the student outsourced the research and writing to another party.

I hope that because you're reading this far into the chapter, I've convinced you that avoiding plagiarism is really the best option. You don't want to risk failing your class as a result of plagiarism. You'll feel lousy about yourself and will have learned nothing, whereas actually doing the assignment yourself will guarantee you an opportunity for growth.

Forms of Plagiarism

What does plagiarism look like? In this section, I'll review four of the most common forms of plagiarism, using the text below as our original source. The examples are fictional text from a student paper.

Primary Source

The '60s: it wasn't just "The Age of Aquarius." It was truly an age of reform and revolution. Mainstream politicians launched a multifaceted campaign to eliminate poverty, expand government services to the elderly, and increase educational opportunities for people of all ages.

Over the course of the decade, Congress passed historic legislation transforming the role of government in American society. The Civil Rights Acts of 1964, the Voting Rights Act of 1965, Medicare, Medicaid, Head Start, the Job Corps, the Office of Economic Opportunity, the Department of Housing and Urban Development, and the Department of Transportation were all part of this legislative record.

But reform was not confined to the Washington political establishment. Student activists rallied to fight racial segregation and end the Vietnam War. Much of this protest was peaceful. Students cited the examples set by Gandhi and Martin Luther King, Jr. in seeking nonviolent social change.

But some activists lost confidence in nonviolent methods as the decade passed and the war in Vietnam continued. Radical factions like the Weathermen argued that the war abroad and racial and class injustices at home required more aggressive responses. By the end of the decade, these militants had gone underground to wage a campaign of targeted bombings against government institutions linked to the war and "oppression."[12]

12. "The 1960s Introduction," Shmoop Study Guides, accessed March 30, 2025, https://www.shmoop.com/study-guides/1960s/.

- Direct plagiarism.

As you might guess from the label, direct plagiarism involves copying text directly from another source without attribution, with no quotation or citation provided.[5]

5 "The Common Types of Plagiarism," Office of the Dean of Students, Bowdoin College, accessed January 20, 2025, https://www.bowdoin.edu/dean-of-students/conduct-review-board.

Example: The 1960s was a decade of reform. Over the course of the decade, Congress passed historic legislation transforming the role of government in American society.

Since this example has no citation, and the source contains a sentence written exactly as it appears in the original text, this constitutes direct plagiarism. Had the student put the second sentence in quotation marks and cited the source in a footnote, it would no longer be an example of plagiarism.

- Mosaic plagiarism.

Mosaic plagiarism occurs when a student takes phrases directly from an original without quoting the source, or mimics the sentence structure of the original source while replacing key terms with synonyms. This is plagiarism even if a citation to the original is included. It is sometimes called "patch writing."[6]

Example A: Government leaders staged a complex battle to eradicate poverty, broadened federal assistance to senior citizens, and enhanced learning opportunities for American citizens of every demographic. (note)

At first glance, this might appear to be a decent paraphrase of the original. But if you look closely, it is actually a plagiarized version of the second sentence above, as the original structure is maintained. Mosaic plagiarism in this case resulted from the student's mistakes in paraphrasing, as they did not change the structure of the original text.

Example B: The government and American citizens played major roles in bringing about reform in the 1960s. Congress passed historic legislation, "transforming the role of government in American society." Student activists got involved, too. They rallied to fight racial segregation. Other Americans lost confidence in nonviolent methods. (note)

The writer attempts to put original language in quotation marks and cites the source they are referring to. But the writer has also used phrases

6 "The Common Types of Plagiarism," Office of the Dean of Students, Bowdoin College.

from the original text without placing them in quotation marks, such as "Congress passed historic legislation," "rallied to fight racial segregation," and "lost confidence in nonviolent methods." While it would seem from this example that the writer did not intend to plagiarize, given their inclusion of a citation, this can still be regarded as plagiarism.

- Self-plagiarism.

Self-plagiarism refers to a case in which a student re-uses their own work for a new assignment. You might ask why this counts as plagiarism if the student wrote the original material. For every assignment in college, you're expected to do the work *at the time it's assigned, and in the framework of a particular course and a particular semester*. You also can't submit something for your history course that you are working on for another course, even if you're taking it at the same time. If you are interested on building upon something you've done in the past for another course, it might be a different story. The best thing to do if you are unsure is to ask your professor ahead of time if your plan is acceptable. If you wish to study a topic that is very close to something you're doing in another course this semester, then get permission from both instructors before pursuing that path.[7]

It's also important to recognize that plagiarism detection software like Turnitin.com includes in its database all previous work that students have submitted on the web. So, if you had to turn in something in the past, your "new" (or not so new) paper will come up as plagiarized.

- Accidental plagiarism (misuse of sources).

A fourth type of plagiarism is what results when students don't intend to plagiarize but end up doing so because they are careless in the way they take notes and write their papers. They may forget to cite a source, paraphrase in a way that is too close to the original text, or cite a source inadequately. It's characterized among the forms of plagiarism because from the instructor's standpoint, it raises the same set of issues, despite the fact that the student did not necessarily know they were making a mistake.[8] In many ways there is considerable overlap between mosaic plagiarism and accidental plagiarism.

7 "The Common Types of Plagiarism," Office of the Dean of Students, Bowdoin College.
8 "The Common Types of Plagiarism," Office of the Dean of Students, Bowdoin College.

How Instructors Detect Plagiarism

In addition to the many software packages that help instructors identify potential cases of plagiarism, professors also see red flags in student writing that frequently suggest a problem.

The paper uses inconsistent citation styles. When a paper shifts back and forth between several citation styles, it suggests that the paper has been copied from several different sources.

The paper contains passages of unusually clear and eloquent writing, without citation. While many students write well, few college students are such masterful writers that they sound like they've had professional editors working with them. Turns of phrase that seem unusually eloquent, as well as vocabulary that is not consistent with the student's own writing style, suggest plagiarism. Sometimes, the change in style is very abrupt, allowing the instructor to see where the student's writing stopped and the plagiarized writing began. And if a student who has seemed checked out from the course (as in the third scenario under "Why Students Plagiarize," above) suddenly produces a highly polished-looking paper, that in itself can be a red flag.

The paper goes off-topic or fails to develop ideas in the order one would expect. Students who plagiarize do not go through the writing process in a logical fashion. Instead, they steal several decent passages that seem like they could touch on their topic of study. That comes across as a narrative that fails to develop along an expected trajectory.

The paper has few specific time references, or seems out of date. A lack of this type of data suggests a paper recycled from another student or generated by a paper mill.

"Smoking guns." Sometimes, the student is so rushed, or so careless, as to basically announce to the reader, "Yes, this is plagiarized, and here's the original." In classes I taught, students included hyperlinks to the original paper; the original author's name; and—one of my personal favorites—the student's own name with last year's date at the top of the page.[9]

Googling a sentence from the paper. Instructors can simply Google a sentence and find the originals of plagiarized passages.

---

9 For more on "smoking guns," see Robert Harris, "Anti-Plagiarism Strategies for Research Papers," VirtualSalt, February 28, 2012, https://students.umw.edu/chls/files/2012/10/Anti-Plagiarism-Strategies1.pdf. See also "Resources for Teachers: How to Detect Plagiarism," MIT Comparative Media Studies/Writing, Massachusetts Institute of Technology, accessed January 20, 2025, https://cmsw.mit.edu/writing-and-communication-center.

Avoiding Plagiarism

In my experience, most students have good intentions regarding academic integrity and do not begin the semester thinking they can get away with plagiarism. But good intentions can only go so far if you don't know how to incorporate or credit sources. Here are some basic rules about when sources must be cited.

You need to cite a source any time you quote, paraphrase, or summarize. There's a widespread myth that sources only need to be cited when they are quoted directly. No! That is completely wrong. If the ideas are not your own—whether or not you are using the precise words—you must provide a citation.

You don't need to cite a source if the information provided constitutes "common knowledge." What does this mean? Generally, "common knowledge" refers to "information generally known to an educated reader, such as widely known facts and dates, and more rarely, ideas or language."[10] If you can find the fact in several general encyclopedias, it is probably okay not to cite it. But if it's a fact that might only be known to someone who is familiar with a certain discipline, you should cite it. When in doubt, cite the source.

Here are three of the most common reasons that students misuse sources:

- Sloppy notetaking skills.
- Lack of experience with proper paraphrasing.
- Lack of experience integrating sources into academic writing.

I should be clear from the start. No single research guide is going to teach you everything you need to know about using sources properly and avoiding plagiarism. You have to practice, just as you would an instrument or a sport. You'll find it easier after you have done it a few times the right way. But I can at least get you started. Below are some pointers that address each of the three problems above. If you keep these pointers in mind, you will go a long way toward avoiding accidental plagiarism.

Steer clear of notetaking mistakes:

- When you are quoting word-for-word, use quotation marks, or put the quotation in a distinct color. You need to do this so you

10 "The Exception: Common Knowledge," Harvard College Writing Program, Harvard University, accessed January 20, 2025, https://usingsources.fas.harvard.edu/.

won't accidentally cut and paste a direct quotation into your paper.

- Get into the habit of summarizing and paraphrasing when you are taking notes from sources. Keep direct quotations to a minimum.
- When taking notes, write down the source and page number regularly, so it is easy to find the original later if you need to go back to it.
- Distinguish your own ideas or comments on sources from the ideas of authors by using a different font or highlighting them.
- Remember that every time you quote, summarize, or paraphrase someone else's ideas, you need to include a source citation in the form of a footnote or endnote.

Paraphrase properly:

- Read a passage several times and then close the book or the document. In your head, try to articulate the main point of the passage in your own words. Then write down what you've come up with.
- Remember that a paraphrase must *differ in structure* from the original sentence or passage. You can't simply write the same sentence and substitute a few of your own words for the author's words.

Integrate your sources into your own writing. The main idea here is to make it clear when you are speaking, and when you are referring to a source (either through summary, paraphrase, or quotation). Remember that you control the narrative of your paper, and the sources you're citing serve your argument. Students frequently forget that and allow the sources to appear randomly, leading to confusion as to which words are the author's. For guidelines on how to integrate sources clearly and effectively, you can review the previous chapter.

See Online Companion Exercises 15A, B, and C
sites.broadviewpress.com/puzzle/chapter-15

Using Artificial Intelligence

In the last few years, the issue of plagiarism in college and university courses has been intensified and complicated even further by the explosion of generative artificial intelligence. Generative AI platforms, of which ChatGPT has garnered the most mainstream attention, are tools that are capable of producing human-like responses to textual prompts that we give them: "Tell me a fun fact about the Ming Dynasty," "Give me five tips to help with procrastination," "Give me a realistic photograph of a skydiving frog." Simply put, these AI platforms "generate" content—text, images, video, code, and so forth—based on the truly massive amount of data that they've been trained on. Large language models (LLMs) such as ChatGPT seize text data from entire books, articles, and websites, which can amount to more than 200 trillion words in total, sometimes more. When prompted, the models refer to this enormous well of data and use it to predict the most apt response. The purpose of generative AI is to create new *content*, not simply to access currently existing content.

AI platforms can do an astonishingly quick job of providing us with all kinds of information or answers to questions. They can give us recipes to use up the items we have in our fridge, compose emails, write code or suggest spreadsheet formulas, create charts and tables, find data sets, suggest travel plans, and so on. And as you may be discovering, they can also produce a readymade, complete essay based on a single prompt with very little effort on the part of the individual providing the prompt.

In short, AI produces a "thing," an output. Crucially, though, what it *doesn't* do is provide the process—that is, it doesn't provide the very thing from which we *learn*. Nor, of course, does it understand what it's doing, which can introduce problems. And because all it does is comb through a gigantic repository of preexisting text and use it to generate a plausible-sounding response to a prompt or query, AI does not—and, at the time of writing, cannot—produce *new* knowledge or a *new* interpretation of existing knowledge. (It's worth reemphasizing that in light of what I just said about generative AI's purpose being to create new content: new *content* is not the same thing as new *knowledge*.) **Your primary objective in completing a research project—identifying a new or fresh interpretation of a historical event—remains beyond AI's capacities.**

When used thoughtfully and responsibly, generative AI can be tremendously helpful with the researching and writing of a history paper. Here are guiding questions that can help you make appropriate choices about when and how to use AI.

- What is the purpose (or reason) you are turning to AI for your research project?
  - How am I using AI? Am I using it to brainstorm? To help me find some relevant sources or keywords for research? To help me better understand a confusing concept? To summarize or better organize my notes?
  - Am I asking it to write something for me from scratch?
  - How might I be cheating myself by taking a shortcut through AI?

As these questions suggest, AI can be an invaluable resource **for discovering new sources or terms, or for organizing information**. You'll run into trouble, however, if you expect AI to do the writing, thinking, or interpretation of sources for you.

- Am I using AI to create something *new* for my research project?
  - Am I the sole creator of what I'm handing in?
  - Could AI be considered the creator or co-creator, in part or in whole, *in any way whatsoever*?
  - Have I acknowledged and cited where and how I have used AI?

If you take the words or images that AI produces and use them as your own, it is plagiarism, and is it no different from copying word for word from any other source. If you did not produce the work that you are submitting, it isn't yours. Any use of AI, in any capacity, should be acknowledged.

- Am I relying on AI to determine accuracy?
  - Have I verified what AI has produced?
  - Have I double- and triple-checked whether AI has hallucinated any "factual" information, sources, or references?

Despite its name, AI does not *understand* what it is producing; it merely predicts a word, then a next word and a next word, based on the scads of text data it has scanned. There's no actual intelligence, per se, at work in what it does. This is why some AI-generated images that you may have seen have incomplete, nonsensical, or impossible features, and why some AI models invent "facts" and sources that don't actually exist.

For example, when an Australian economist named David Smerdon asked ChatGPT "What is the most cited economics paper of all time?," it simply made up a paper called "A Theory of Economic History," attributing it to two real scholars, Douglass North and Robert Thomas, and claiming that it had been published in a real journal, *The Journal of Economic History*, in 1969.[11] This incident is a good example of how AI models such as ChatGPT work—and of why, appearances to the contrary, they are not alternatives to search engines such as Google. When Smerdon prompted it, ChatGPT did not sift through a database of real economics articles and count how many times they had been cited in other articles, because that is not what it was programmed to do. Rather, it did what it *is* programmed to do, which is draw on an enormous body of pre-existing text to generate a response that looked plausible: a title consisting of a sequence of words—"theory," "economic," and "history"—that it predicted were likely to occur together, attached to the names of real economists and a real economics journal.

In other words, when you ask AI models for information, what they give you is text that has been algorithmically crafted to resemble real information. But what it turns out may or may not be accurate! If you ask an AI model for a full essay, it will predict that certain things that *look* like sources should appear at certain points in the essay and so will provide them—real or not.

- Have I paid attention to the role of bias and misinformation in my use of AI?
  - Have I considered how and on what sources the AI has been trained?
  - Is it possible that AI has produced something that has been sourced from biased (or false) information, and so perpetuates that implicit bias (or falsehood)?

The information that AI provides has been gleaned from whatever original materials it scoured. If these materials were biased, prejudiced, or

11 G. Anandlingam, "The Risks of Unintelligent Adoption of Artificial Intelligence," Network Readiness Index, November 27, 2023, https://networkreadinessindex.org/the-risks-of-unintelligent-adoption-of-artificial-intelligence/.

otherwise not representative, then the information AI produces will necessarily reflect the poor representation. In one 2023 study, for example, the AI model Stable Diffusion, which generates images based on text prompts, was asked to create representations of workers in fourteen jobs, seven of which are typically considered "high-paying" (such as lawyer, engineer, and CEO) and seven of which are typically considered "low-paying" (such as housekeeper, janitor, and fast-food worker). A majority of the images the model generated for every conventionally high-paying job were of lighter-skinned men, whereas most of the images generated for many of the conventionally low-paying jobs were of people with darker skin tones; of the three hundred images generated for the keyword "engineer," only one was of a woman (another was of a person whose gender was ambiguous).[12]

Similarly, the textual archives on which AI models such as ChatGPT are trained include thousands of works, and billions of words, written in the eighteenth, nineteenth, and early twentieth centuries, when prevailing ideas about race, gender, and sexuality were quite different—and, to a significant degree, far more prejudiced—than they are today. An AI model whose predictive algorithm is substantially based on works containing such outmoded racist, sexist, and colonialist ideas can well end up reproducing and perpetuating them.

- How does the AI platform I have chosen regard the issue of privacy?
  - Have I considered who owns the AI and what they're doing with my personal information, my questions and prompts, and any text that I provide it?
  - Is the AI I'm using accessible to everyone? Even if it is, are there any motives behind its availability that I should be aware of?
  - Does the AI use content that is under copyright? If so, have the owners or developers of the AI obtained the consent of the creators whose work the AI is drawing on?

Some AI platforms are open source. ChatGPT began operating as such; its creators believed that this was the only ethical means by which to provide the technology to the public. They have since changed their model and operate

12 Leonardo Nicoletti and Dina Bass, "Humans Are Biased. Generative AI Is Even Worse," Bloomberg, June 9, 2023, https://www.bloomberg.com/graphics/2023-generative-ai-bias/.

now as a private for-profit company. Importantly, many large language models have taken text and images from sources that are in copyright and used them without the creators' consent. When using AI models, then—just as when we use any other product or service—it falls to us as individuals to consider the motives, ethical stances, and behavior of the models' owners. This may influence our willingness to adopt their technology.

- Have I considered both my instructor's and my institution's position and/or policy on the use of AI?

It is increasingly rare for an instructor, department, or institution not to have at least a general policy on the use of AI. This policy should outline the accepted uses of AI and spell out what is considered to be a misuse or abuse of the technology. Your class syllabus is a good place to look to find an official statement spelling out your instructor's policy on AI. If you're unsure, ask your instructor.

- Generative AI technology is changing by the month and will surely grow more versatile or capable within the lifetime of this book, perhaps exponentially so.
  - Are any of the questions above less or more relevant to me and my use of AI?
  - What has changed in AI since I first used it? Does my answer to this question have an impact on my decision on whether to use it today—and how I might use it?

These are just some of the issues that generative AI raises and that anyone who uses it (and even those who don't wish or intend to use it) is obliged to think through. Generative AI seems likely to be as transformative, if not more so, as any of the other great technological innovations in human history—from the internet, through TV, radio, the telephone, the telegraph, and the printing press, back to the invention of writing itself.

For anyone interested in history and historical change—as I hope anyone reading this book is likely to be—the growth of generative AI is thus bound to be an exciting and fascinating phenomenon. At the same time, history teaches that wisdom and discernment are essential for the transformative potential of such innovations to be unlocked in the most useful and beneficial way. By exercising such wisdom and discernment yourself, you can use AI to enrich your historical research and writing.

AFTERWORD

A Note to Students

When I first decided to write about my experience teaching historical research skills, I approached this project from a very different vantage point. At that time, I was primarily concerned with helping students make it from the beginning of the semester to the end. My main objective was giving them the tools they needed to complete the research process and write a decent history paper. I felt confident that if they were patient and didn't cut corners, the skills they learned along the way would benefit them in future history classes as well as elsewhere in the humanities.

At that earlier point in my professional career, this book was for college students taking a particular type of course. The skills taught in the research process had relevance beyond the classroom, of course, and I tried to highlight that whenever necessary. But that wasn't my primary focus.

Now, eight years later, the thought process and analytical skills required to complete a historical research paper seem more important than ever. They are essential to operating as an educated citizen today. A dramatic change occurred in the United States with the election of Donald Trump as president in 2016. Some call that moment the beginning of "post-truth politics." In this new period, political arguments matter more than a commonly agreed upon set of facts. Experts are often shoved to the sidelines. Conspiracy theories reign in not just the darker corners of the internet, but on mainstream sites. For some, fact checkers can't act quickly enough to correct misrepresentations or mistakes. But for others, fact checkers are simply acting out of political interest and can't be trusted.

How are we to navigate the post-truth era? It's surely easiest to do the opposite of everything this book teaches, particularly in the age of memes, soundbites, and information silos. I urge students reading this book to resist the temptation. Easy explanations for complex problems are usually faulty and comically oversimplified.

Never let anyone else tell you what to believe or how to think. Ask questions and draw your own conclusions. Read a variety of sources; listen to and acknowledge others' perspectives. The discipline of History encourages us to cleave to facts and interpretations supported by those facts. Evaluate and question sources, separate reliable information from disinformation, and craft a cohesive argument. Communicate clearly and engage in civil and respectful dialogue across lines of difference. In doing so, you'll start to solve the puzzle of today's political fractures and polarization just as you did when crafting an interpretation of the past.

Index

About the Publisher

The word "broadview" expresses a good deal of the philosophy behind our company. Our focus is very much on the humanities and social sciences—especially literature, writing, and philosophy—but within these fields we are open to a broad range of academic approaches and political viewpoints. We strive in particular to produce high-quality, pedagogically useful books for higher education classrooms—anthologies, editions, sourcebooks, surveys of particular academic fields and sub-fields, and also course texts for subjects such as composition, business communication, and critical thinking. We welcome the perspectives of authors from marginalized and underrepresented groups, and we have a strong commitment to the environment. We publish English-language works and translations from many parts of the world, and our books are available world-wide; we also publish a select list of titles with a specifically Canadian emphasis.

broadview press

The interior of this book is printed on 100% recycled paper.